Certification Guide

Eighth Edition

HUMAN RESOURCE CERTIFICATION INSTITUTE

Certification Guide

Eighth Edition

Raymond B. Weinberg, SPHR, CCP

CERTIFICATION INSTITUTE
SOCIETY FOR HUMAN RESOURCE MANAGEMENT

This book is published by the Human Resource Certification Institute (HRCI®).

© 1982, 2004 Human Resource Certification Institute
1800 Duke Street, Alexandria, VA 22314

The Human Resource Certification Institute (HRCI) is the credentialing organization founded by the Society for Human Resource Management (SHRM) to promote the establishment of professional standards both domestically and globally. HRCI recognizes HR professionals who, through demonstrated professional experience and the passing of a comprehensive exam, have met HRCI's requirements for mastering the HR body of knowledge. Established in 1976, today, HRCI recognizes more than 65,000 HR professionals with active PHR and SPHR designations. Visit HRCI online at **www.hrci.org**.

ISBN 1-58644-050-0

Printed in the United States of America
10 9 8 7 6 5 4 3 2 1

Table of Contents

Preface

To stay current in the human resource (HR) management field, individuals must continually update their knowledge and skills. The 21st century U.S. workplace will require HR professionals to respond to such widely varying concerns as the changing nature of work, re-engineered workplaces, virtual offices, the boundary-less organization, employee rights, worker literacy, and global competition—to name just a few.

As the profession changes, so does the body of knowledge that HR professionals must master. Consequently, through extensive research conducted by the Human Resource Certification Institute (HRCI), efforts to identify the domestic HR body of knowledge have been undertaken. From this process, new and revised test specifications are developed and updated in all HR functional areas. These specifications form the blueprint for development of the HRCI certification exams.

HRCI's mission is to serve the professional and advance the profession by providing excellence in human resource certification. Depending on experience levels, individuals in the profession can attain certification as either a Professional in Human Resources (PHR) or a Senior Professional in Human Resources (SPHR). This guide is an aid to candidates considering taking one of these exams. It is designed to help candidates understand the certification process, allow them to assess their levels of preparedness and determine which areas may need additional review.

Acknowledgments

This publication would not have been possible without the contribution of the HRCI Board of Directors and the many volunteers who help in item and exam development. It is the work of these dedicated volunteers that is the basis for the content of this publication.

Volunteers are the heart of HRCI's certification program. All are certified professionals who have successfully passed the exams. They write and review draft test items, establish passing or cut scores, and otherwise support the Institute in its mission.

SECTION I:

The PHR and SPHR Certification Guide

This guide was developed with a number of purposes in mind. First, it was designed to provide HR professionals with relevant information about HRCI and its certification process. Second, it describes the Institute's practice analysis process and its outcome—test specifications based on the domestic human resource management body of knowledge. Third, it explains various ways to prepare for the PHR or SPHR exam. Finally, it provides sample test questions so individuals can assess their mastery of the domestic HR body of knowledge.

There are two primary reasons why HR professionals are reluctant to take the HRCI certification exams. First, there is fear of the unknown, such as not knowing what to study or what types of questions will be asked. Another closely related reason is the fear of failure—not knowing one's level of proficiency before taking the exam. These two fears, whether real or imagined, prevent many capable HR professionals from taking one of the certification exams. This book was designed to alleviate these fears.

This publication is a starting point for formal training or informal self-development for HR professionals interested in individual or group study in the human resource management field.

Copies of the *PHR and SPHR Certification Guide* may be purchased from the SHRMStore, PO Box 930132, Atlanta, GA 31193-0132, (800) 444-5006 or ordered online at shrmstore.shrm.org. This book can also be purchased through Amazon and Barnes and Noble. Proceeds from the sales of this book are used to support the educational purposes and operations of the Institute. Inquiries about the certification program may be addressed to:

Human Resource Certification Institute
1800 Duke Street
Alexandria, VA 22314
(866) 898-HRCI (4724)
Fax: (703) 535-6474
TTY/TDD: (703) 548-6999
E-mail: info@hrci.org
HRCI Web site: www.hrci.org

SECTION II:

Human Resource Professionalism

In the mid-1960s, the American Society for Personnel Administration (now the Society for Human Resource Management) and Cornell University asked the U.S. Department of Labor a simple question—"What constitutes a profession?" The Department of Labor said there were five distinct characteristics that separate a profession from other pursuits or endeavors:

1. National Organization—A profession is defined by the existence of a national organization that can speak as a unified voice for its members and foster the development of the field. The Society for Human Resource Management (SHRM), with a membership exceeding 175,000, fulfills that role for the human resource management profession.

2. Code of Ethics—A profession has a code of ethics that identifies standards of behavior relating to fairness, justice, truthfulness, and social responsibility. SHRM has developed such a code to which all members are expected to adhere.

   HRCI has also developed the following Model of Professional Excellence that includes ethical standards:

   HRCI Model of Professional Excellence

   As certified human resource professionals, our personal standards of honor and integrity must, at all times, be above reproach and we must conduct ourselves in a manner that reflects favorably on our profession.

By adhering to the highest standard of honor and integrity, we as human resource professionals help create an ethical climate within our organizations.

We have a duty to protect the interests of our employees, the organization and the society to promote and encourage:

- Honesty and trustworthiness in all working relationships.
- Reliability in performing our assigned responsibilities.
- Truthfulness and accuracy in what is said and written.
- Constructiveness and cooperation in working relationships.
- Fairness, consideration, and nondiscrimination in how we treat others.
- Adherence to the law in all activities.
- Economical use of resources.
- Commitment to excellence in the performance of our work.
- Respect for the privacy of others.

3. Research—A profession is also marked by the existence of applied research related to the field. The SHRM Foundation funds research into new and emerging areas of HR. HRCI provides financial support to the SHRM Foundation in its pursuit of advancing the HR field. In 2000, SHRM established a dedicated research department.

4. Body of Knowledge—A profession has a defined body of knowledge. HRCI, through its practice analysis study, defines the domestic HR body of knowledge. This body of knowledge (the basis of the Institute's test specifications) is disseminated to professionals through publications, many of which are sponsored by SHRM.

5. Credentialing—Lastly, a profession has a credentialing organization that sets professional standards in the field. HRCI fulfills this requirement.

Together, SHRM, the SHRM Foundation and HRCI meet the requirements that define the human resource field as a profession. Although still developing, the high standards set by these organizations, plus the high level of performance expected of an HR professional, will make the challenge of professionalism that much greater in the future.

Human Resource Certification Institute

HRCI develops and maintains professional standards in the HR field. This is accomplished by defining and periodically updating the domestic HR body of knowledge, promoting self-development of HR professionals, and recognizing and credentialing those who have met established experience requirements and have demonstrated mastery of the domestic HR body of knowledge by passing one of the HRCI exams.

The first certification exams were administered in the spring of 1976 following years of extensive work by a task force formed by SHRM, then known as the American Society for Personnel Administration. Their efforts resulted in a certification program open to professionals in the HR field.

Today, HRCI is governed by a volunteer board of directors composed of certified HR professionals dedicated to advancing the professionalism in the field. Item writing, item review and exam review panels (also comprised of volunteers) write test questions, review the body of knowledge test specifications and bibliographic reference lists, and review exam forms. HRCI employs a highly qualified staff to administer its certification program.

PHR and SPHR Certification

HRCI offers two exams developed for HR professionals responsible for domestic HR issues—the Professional in Human Resources (PHR) exam and the Senior Professional in Human Resources (SPHR) exam. In addition, HRCI offers an exam developed for HR professionals responsible for international HR issues—the Global Professional in Human Resources (GPHR™) exam. However, this guide was developed only for the PHR and SPHR exams.

To be eligible to take either the PHR or SPHR exam, candidates must have two years of exempt-level (professional) HR experience. The PHR exam focuses more on the technical and operational aspects of HR. The SPHR exam focuses on strategic HR policy issues.

Candidates should select the certification level they feel best represents their mastery of the domestic HR body of knowledge. Candidate performance has shown that appropriate exempt-level (professional) HR work experience and educational background contributes significantly to the likelihood of success on the exams. It is strongly recommended that PHR candidates have two to four years of exempt-level (professional) HR experience and that SPHR candidates have six to eight years of exempt-level (professional) HR experience. Success depends on mastery of the entire body of knowledge as reflected in the test specifications. Therefore, candidates should carefully assess their qualifications (using the guidelines discussed above) before selecting the certification exam level.

Choosing the Right Exam Level

An honest assessment of skills, knowledge and responsibilities within the HR function is critical when deciding which exam to take. The following profiles of typical PHR and SPHR candidates may help you decide which level is right for you.

The ideal PHR candidate:

- Focuses on program implementation.
- Has tactical/logistical orientation.
- Has accountability to another HR professional within the organization.
- Has two to four years of exempt-level (professional) generalist HR work experience, but because of career length, may lack the breadth and depth of a more senior-level generalist.
- Has not had progressive HR work experience by virtue of career length.
- Focuses his or her affect on the organization within the HR department rather than organizationwide.
- Commands respect through the credibility of knowledge and the use of policies and guidelines to make decisions.

The ideal SPHR candidate:

- Designs and plans rather than implements.
- Focuses on the "big picture."
- Has ultimate accountability in the HR department.
- Has six to eight years of progressive HR experience.
- Has breadth and depth of HR generalist knowledge.
- Uses judgment obtained with time and application of knowledge.
- Is not specialized; has generalist role within organization.
- Understands the affect of decisions within and outside of the organization.
- Understands the business, not just the HR function.
- Manages relationships; has influence within overall organization.
- Commands credibility within organization, community and field by experience.
- Possesses excellent negotiation skills.
- Operates invisibly.

The HRCI Assessment Exam

HRCI now offers an online assessment exam for the PHR and SPHR exams. Potential candidates can use this exam to assess their knowledge level before taking the actual exam. The assessment exams were developed using actual test questions from previous exams and will give candidates a chance to become familiar with the format of the exam questions and determine their readiness for the actual exam. Before registering for the exam, consider investing in the assessment exam. For more information, visit the HRCI Web site at www.hrci.org.

Eligibility as a Student or Recent Graduate

Students may take the PHR certification exam even though they lack the required two years of exempt-level (professional) HR experience. To qualify in this category, candidates must not meet the work experience requirements necessary to take the PHR exam. Students and recent graduates are permitted to take the exam no earlier than 12 months before their graduation date and recent graduates no later than 12 months after their graduation date. Students/recent graduates have five years from the date of passing the exam to secure the required exempt-level HR (professional) work experience. After meeting the experience requirement, students/recent graduates must:

- Provide documentation of graduation.
- Submit documentation outlining the required work experience.
- Pay the balance of the certification fee.

Student/recent graduate candidates who take and pass the exam may not use the PHR designation until they have met the work experience requirement. Candidates qualifying as a student/recent graduate are not eligible to take the SPHR certification exam.

Definitions

The PHR and SPHR exams are developed for HR professionals who are currently working at an exempt (professional) level in the HR field. While that work need not always be exclusively in HR, the majority (51 percent) of a person's daily activities must be within the human resource function. Therefore, the following general definitions apply when assessing eligibility:

Practitioner: One whose duties are those normally found in the typical HR function.

Educator: One whose principal area of instruction is in the HR field in an accredited institution of higher education.

Researcher: One whose research activities are restricted primarily to the HR field.

Consultant: One whose consulting activities are predominantly in the HR field.

Use of Certification

HRCI certifications are voluntary and conferred by HRCI solely when an HR professional has demonstrated achievement of national standards by passing the PHR, SPHR or GPHR exam. Persons or organizations choosing to incorporate PHR, SPHR or GPHR certification as a condition of employment or advancement do so of their own volition. Candidates must determine for themselves whether the use of such a certification process, including its eligibility and recertification requirements, when coupled with other requirements imposed by such persons, meets their needs and complies with applicable laws.

Applications

HRCI publishes the *PHR and SPHR Certification Handbook* annually. This handbook provides information about the certification process and eligibility requirements and includes an application form (not included in the online version). It includes the current exam fee schedule and test center locations. The handbook is available online at www.hrci.org or upon request. To request a hard copy, write, e-mail or phone HRCI:

> Human Resource Certification Institute
> 1800 Duke Street
> Alexandria, VA 22314
> (866) 898-4724
> Fax: (703) 535-6474
> TTY/TDD: (703) 548-6999
> E-mail: info@hrci.org

Candidates should refer only to the most recent handbook as HRCI may change or modify policies and procedures from year to year. Similarly, only the most current application form should be used.

PHR and SPHR Recertification

Certification demonstrates mastery of the domestic HR body of knowledge in an increasingly demanding field. As every HR professional knows, however, the field is in constant flux. HR professionals who strive to maintain their professional edge must keep up with the rapid change and new dimensions that define the profession. Recertification demonstrates that certified professionals have stayed abreast of change and updated their HR knowledge.

Recertification is required within three years of passing the exam. Each subsequent recertification period is also for three years. There are two ways to recertify:

Recertification by Exam

All requirements for recertification may be met by passing the current, applicable exam. Candidates choosing this option must take the exam at the same designation level before their certification cycle expires. For more information about this method of recertification, please contact HRCI at (866) 898-4724 or info@hrci.org or visit the HRCI Web site at www.hrci.org.

Recertification by Updating Education and Experience

Recertification through professional development and experience can be achieved by accumulating 60 credit hours during a recertification cycle. Credit hours can be achieved through a variety of methods. Please refer to the latest recertification brochure and application (distributed by HRCI or available at www.hrci.org) for more information on the number of credit hours allowed per category.

Continuing Education: Recertification credit can be earned by participating in HR-related courses, workshops, seminars or conferences. All 60 recertification credit hours can be obtained in this category.

Research and/or Publishing: Recertification credit can be earned by conducting an HR-related research project or by writing and publishing in the HR field. Writing an article for a newsletter will not meet this requirement. A maximum of 20 recertification credit hours can be obtained in this category.

Instruction: Recertification candidates can earn credit hours by preparing for and teaching a new college-level class or making a presentation at a workshop or conference (including in-house training programs). Credits can be earned only for the first time the presentation is made. A maximum of 20 recertification credit hours can be obtained in this category.

On the Job: Certain projects at work can earn recertification credit. A first-time work activity that adds to the candidate's HR knowledge base can be credited. The focus in this area is to capture new knowledge. A maximum of 20 recertification credit hours can be obtained in this category.

Leadership: HR professionals can earn recertification credit hours through leadership responsibilities in an HR professional organization such as SHRM at a national, area, state or local level or in a civic/community activity where HR knowledge is the primary reason for the affiliation. A maximum of 10 recertification credit hours can be obtained in this category.

Professional Membership: Up to 10 recertification credit hours (over a three-year recertification cycle) for professionals who are members of a national HR organization such as SHRM.

Recertification Application and Fees

Application forms for recertification through professional development are available from HRCI and can be downloaded from the HRCI Web site at www.hrci.org. Recertification-by-exam candidates can request a paper form from HRCI at (866) 868-4724, through the HRCI Web site (www.hrci.org), or by e-mail at info@hrci.org. Recertification-by-exam candidates can also apply for the exam online.

SECTION III:
The Domestic HR Body of Knowledge

Defining the Domestic HR Body of Knowledge

What should a human resource practitioner know and be able to apply to be considered a competent HR generalist? This is the fundamental question HRCI seeks to answer through its practice analysis study, an extensive research program specifically designed to define and update the domestic HR body of knowledge.

The HR field is dynamic and in a constant state of change. Consequently, the knowledge requirements must reflect these changes. The practice analysis process keeps HR knowledge requirements both relevant and up to date.

To set standards for the credentialing of a profession, the relevant body of knowledge must first be defined. The domestic HR body of knowledge is the foundation upon which HRCI's PHR and SPHR certification program is built. From this body of knowledge, test specifications are developed. In turn, these specifications are used as a blueprint for the PHR and SPHR exams. Exam items are developed to measure the knowledge requirements that reflect the topics in the test specifications.

The end result of this research is a set of assurances that PHR and SPHR certifications are:

- Based on a set of well-defined knowledge requirements.
- Current and able to respond to rapid changes in the field.
- Based on "real-life" human resource management practices.
- Focused on important knowledge and not trivial matters.

Codification research to define the HR body of knowledge began in 1976 with a group of HR professionals from throughout the United States. Their roles were to critique draft content outlines and weightings, recommend revisions, suggest sources for bibliographies and make other pertinent comments.

To revise the content outlines, a modified Delphi technique involving hundreds of professionals was used in 1979 and in 1984. This method used a multiple nomination technique to identify experts who were widely known and respected as HR leaders. These experts included practitioners, educators, researchers and consultants. They were asked to perform a highly detailed evaluation of the content outlines and bibliographies. Statistical analyses were performed. The resulting body of knowledge represented the consensus views of those experts.

Before 1988, the practice analysis methodology used HR experts for a normative (or what the field ought to be) perspective. In 1988, HRCI (then known as the Personnel Accreditation Institute) went to the "real" experts in the HR field for a descriptive (the way it is) perspective. More than 41,000 human resource practitioners, educators, researchers and consultants received a detailed questionnaire of 234 separate items. Participants were asked to evaluate each of the questions in terms of how essential it was to their particular job. In addition, a number of demographic factors were asked to allow for more in-depth analyses of data.

The HRCI board and SHRM committee chairs gathered the data from the questionnaire. That data was then compiled into a comprehensive content outline that served as the foundation for the 1988 HRCI content outline.

HRCI underwent an equally extensive process in 1997 and 2000 and updated the content outline (now known as test specifications). The new test specifications went into effect on January 1, 2002.

To verify and revise test specifications between major surveys, HRCI uses expert reviews, extensive literature searches, and analyses of HR textbooks. This kind of environmental scan identifies new knowledge requirements and those that may be obsolete. Environmental scans took place in 1992 and 1996.

The current test specifications are the basis for certification testing and for the preparation of these publications/products (this is not an exhaustive list):
- HRCI® PHR and SPHR Certification Handbook
- HRCI® Certification Guide
- SHRM® Learning System

The domestic HR body of knowledge is constantly changing. Consequently, the Institute's research in this area is ongoing to ensure that the test specifications and exams reflect current HR knowledge and practices.

PHR and SPHR Test Specifications

The PHR and SPHR exams are divided into functional areas. The weighting of each area is based on its relative importance to the knowledge requirements of an HR generalist. The PHR and SPHR exams are weighted accordingly:

	PHR	SPHR
Strategic Management	12%	26%
Workforce Planning and Employment	26%	16%
Human Resource Development	15%	13%
Compensation and Benefits	20%	16%
Employee and Labor Relations	21%	24%
Occupational Health, Safety and Security	6%	5%

The numbers indicate the percentage composition for each major functional area. The first number is the PHR percentage and the second number is the SPHR percentage.

The numbers in parentheses below indicate the percentage composition for each major functional area. The first number is the PHR percentage and the second number is the SPHR percentage.

01. Strategic Management (12%, 26%)

The processes and activities used to formulate HR objectives, practices, and policies to meet the short- and long-range organizational needs and opportunities, to guide and lead the change process and to evaluate HR's contributions to organizational effectiveness.

Responsibilities:

1. Interpret information related to the organization's operations from internal sources, including financial/accounting, marketing, operations, information technology, and individual employees, in order to participate in strategic planning and policy-making.

2. Interpret information related to the general business environment, industry practices and developments, and technological developments from external sources (for example, publications, government documents, media, and trade organizations) in order to participate in strategic planning and policy-making.

3. Participate as a partner in the organization's strategic planning process.

4. Establish strategic relationships with individuals in the organization, to influence organizational decision-making.

5. Establish relationships/alliances with key individuals in the community and in professional capacities to assist in meeting the organization's strategic needs.

6. Evaluate HR's contribution to organizational effectiveness, including assessment, design, implementation, and evaluation of activities with respect to strategic and organizational measurement in HR objectives.

7. Provide direction and guidance during changes in organizational processes, operations, planning, intervention, leadership training and culture that balances the expectations and needs of the organization, its employees, and other stakeholders (including customers).

8. Develop and shape organizational policy related to the organization's management of its human resources.

9. Cultivate leadership and ethical values in self and others through modeling and teaching.

10. Provide information for the organizational budgeting process, including budget development and review.

11. Monitor legislative environment for proposed changes in law and take appropriate action to support, modify, or stop the proposed action (for example, write to a Member of Congress, provide expert testimony at a public hearing, lobby legislators).

Knowledge:
1. Lawmaking and administrative regulatory processes.
2. Internal and external environmental scanning techniques.
3. Strategic planning process and implementation.
4. Organizational social responsibility (for example, welfare to work, philanthropy, alliances with community-based organizations).
5. Management functions, including planning, organizing, directing, and controlling.
6. Techniques to sustain creativity and innovation.

02. Workforce Planning and Employment (26%, 16%)

The processes of planning, developing, implementing, administering, and performing ongoing evaluation of recruiting, hiring, orientation, and organizational exit to ensure that the workforce will meet the organization's goals and objectives.

Responsibilities:
1. Identify staffing requirements to meet the goals and objectives of the organization.

2. Conduct job analyses to write job descriptions and develop job competencies.
3. Identify and document the essential job functions for positions.
4. Establish hiring criteria based on the competencies needed.
5. Assess internal workforce, labor market, and recruitment agencies to determine the availability of qualified applicants.
6. Identify internal and external recruitment methods and implement them within the context of the organization's goals and objectives.
7. Develop strategies to market the organization to potential applicants.
8. Establish selection procedures, including interviewing, testing, and reference and background checking.
9. Implement selection procedures, including interviewing, testing, and reference and background checking.
10. Develop and/or extend employment offers.
11. Perform or administer post-offer employment activities (for example, employment agreements, completion of I-9 verification form, relocation agreements, and medical exams).
12. Facilitate and/or administer the process by which non-U.S. citizens can legally work in the United States.
13. Design, facilitate, and/or conduct the orientation process, including review of performance standards for new hires and transfers.
14. Evaluate selection and employment processes for effectiveness and implement changes if indicated (for example, employee retention).
15. Develop a succession planning process.
16. Develop and implement the organizational exit process, including unemployment insurance claim responses (includes severance, turnover and outplacement).
17. Develop, implement, manage, and evaluate affirmative action program(s), as may be required.

Knowledge:
7. Federal/state/local employment-related laws (for example, Title VII, ADA, ADEA, Vietnam Veterans, WARN) and regulations (for example, EEOC Uniform Guidelines on Employee Selection Procedures).
8. Immigration law (for example, visas, I-9).
9. Quantitative analyses required to assess past and future staffing needs (for example, cost benefit analysis, costs per hire, selection ratios, adverse impact).
10. Recruitment methods and sources.

11. Staffing alternatives (for example, telecommuting, outsourcing).
12. Planning techniques (for example, succession planning, forecasting).
13. Reliability and validity of selection tests/tools/methods.
14. Use and interpretation of selection tests (for example, psychological/personality, cognitive, and motor/physical assessments).
15. Interviewing techniques.
16. Relocation practices.
17. Impact of compensation and benefits plans on recruitment and retention.
18. International HR and implications of international workforce for workforce planning and employment.
19. Downsizing and outplacement.
20. Internal workforce planning and employment policies, practices, and procedures.

03. Human Resource Development (15%, 13%)

The processes of ensuring that the skills, knowledge, abilities, and performance of the workforce meet the current and future organizational and individual needs through developing, implementing, and evaluating activities and programs addressing employee training and development, change and performance management, and the unique needs of particular employee groups.

Responsibilities:
1. Conduct needs analyses to identify and establish priorities regarding human resource development activities.
2. Develop training programs.
3. Implement training programs.
4. Evaluate training programs.
5. Develop programs to assess employees' potential for growth and development in the organization.
6. Implement programs to assess employees' potential for growth and development in the organization.
7. Evaluate programs to assess employees' potential for growth and development in the organization.
8. Develop change management programs and activities.
9. Implement change management programs and activities.
10. Evaluate change management programs and activities.
11. Develop performance management programs and procedures.
12. Implement performance management programs and procedures.

13. Evaluate performance management programs and procedures.
14. Develop programs to meet the unique needs of particular employees (for example, work/family programs, diversity programs, outplacement programs, repatriation programs, and fast-track programs).
15. Implement programs to meet the unique needs of particular employees (for example, work/family programs, diversity programs, outplacement programs, repatriation programs, and fast-track programs).
16. Evaluate programs to meet the unique needs of particular employees (for example, work/family programs, diversity programs, outplacement programs, repatriation programs, and fast-track programs).

Knowledge:
21. Applicable international, federal, state, and local laws and regulations regarding copyrights and patents.
22. Human resource development theories and applications (including career development and leadership development).
23. Organizational development theories and applications.
24. Training methods, programs, and techniques (design, objectives, methods, etc.).
25. Employee involvement strategies.
26. Task/process analysis.
27. Performance appraisal and performance management methods.
28. Applicable international issues (for example, culture, local management approaches/practices, societal norms).
29. Instructional methods and program delivery (content, building modules of program, selection of presentation/delivery mechanism).
30. Techniques to assess HRD program effectiveness (for example, satisfaction, learning and job performance of program participants, and organizational outcomes such as turnover and productivity).

04. Compensation and Benefits (20%, 16%)

The processes of analyzing, developing, implementing, administering, and performing ongoing evaluation of a total compensation and benefits system for all employee groups consistent with human resource management goals.

Responsibilities:
1. Ensure the compliance of compensation and benefits with applicable federal, state, and local laws (includes IRS rulings).

2. Analyze, develop, implement, and maintain compensation policies and a pay structure consistent with the organization's strategic objectives (includes broad definitions and designs).
3. Analyze and evaluate pay rates based on internal worth and external market conditions (includes wage and salary surveys).
4. Develop/select and implement a payroll system.
5. Administer payroll functions.
6. Evaluate compensation policies to ensure that they are positioning the organization internally and externally according to the organization's strategic objectives.
7. Conduct a benefits plan needs assessment and determine/select the plans to be offered, considering the organization's strategic objectives.
8. Implement and administer benefits plan (addresses more the carrying out of the objectives of the benefits plan).
9. Evaluate benefits program to ensure that it is positioning the organization internally and externally according to the organization's strategic objectives.
10. Analyze, select, implement, maintain, and administer executive compensation, stock purchase, stock options, and incentive and bonus programs (includes profit-sharing).
11. Analyze, develop, select, maintain, and implement expatriate and foreign national compensation and benefits programs.
12. Communicate the compensation and benefits plan and policies to the workforce.

Knowledge:
31. Federal, state, and local compensation and benefits laws (for example, FLSA, ERISA, COBRA).
32. Accounting practices related to compensation and benefits (for example, excess group term life, compensatory time).
33. Job evaluation methods.
34. Job pricing and pay structures.
35. Incentive and variable pay methods.
36. Executive compensation.
37. Noncash compensation methods (for example, stock option plans).
38. Benefits needs analysis.
39. Benefits plans (for example, health insurance, life insurance, pension, education, health club).

40. International compensation laws and practices (for example, expatriate compensation, socialized medicine, mandated retirement).

05. Employee and Labor Relations (21%, 24%)

The processes of analyzing, developing, implementing, administering, and performing ongoing evaluation of the workplace relationship between employer and employee (including the collective bargaining process and union relations) in order to maintain effective relationships and working conditions that balance the employer's needs with the employees' rights in support of the organization's strategic objectives.

Responsibilities:

1. Ensure compliance with all applicable federal, state, and local laws and regulations (catch-all responsibility, including NLRB, ADA, FMLA).
2. Develop and implement employee relations programs that will create a positive organizational culture (most of the legal definitions and general definitions).
3. Promote, monitor, and measure the effectiveness of employee relations activities.
4. Assist in establishing work rules and monitor their application and enforcement to ensure fairness and consistency (for union and nonunion environments).
5. Communicate and ensure understanding by employees of laws, regulations, and organizational policies.
6. Resolve employee complaints filed with federal, state, and local agencies involving employment practices (formal, legal complaints).
7. Develop grievance and disciplinary policies and procedures to ensure fairness and consistency.
8. Implement and monitor grievance and disciplinary policies and procedures to ensure fairness and consistency (includes investigation).
9. Respond to union organizing activity.
10. Participate in collective bargaining activities.

Knowledge:

41. Applicable federal, state and local laws affecting employment in union and nonunion environments, such as antidiscrimination laws, sexual harassment, labor relations and privacy.

42. Techniques for facilitating positive employee relations (for example, small group facilitation, dispute resolution, and labor/management cooperative strategies and programs.

43. Employee involvement strategies (for example, alternate work schedules, work teams).

44. Individual employment rights issues and practices (for example, employment at will, negligent hiring, defamation, employees' rights to bargain collectively).

45. Workplace behavior issues/practices (for example, absenteeism, discipline).

46. Methods for assessment of employee attitudes, opinions and satisfaction (for example, opinion surveys, attitude surveys, focus panels).

47. Unfair labor practices.

48. The collective bargaining process, strategies and concepts (up to and after contract).

49. Public-sector labor relations issues and practices.

50. Expatriation and repatriation issues and practices.

51. Employee and labor relations for local nationals (i.e., labor relations in other countries).

06. Occupational Health, Safety and Security (6%, 5%)

The processes of analyzing, developing, implementing, administering and performing ongoing evaluation of programs, practices and services to promote the physical and mental well-being of individuals in the workplace, and to protect individuals and the workplace from unsafe acts, unsafe working conditions and violence.

Responsibilities:

1. Ensure compliance with all applicable federal, state and local workplace health and safety laws and regulations.

2. Determine safety programs needed for the organization.

3. Develop and/or select injury/occupational illness prevention programs.

4. Implement injury/occupational illness prevention programs.

5. Develop and/or select safety training and incentive programs.

6. Implement safety training and incentive programs.

7. Evaluate the effectiveness of safety prevention, training and incentive programs.

8. Implement workplace injury/occupational illness procedures (for example, workers' compensation, OSHA).
9. Determine health and wellness programs needed for the organization.
10. Develop/select, implement and evaluate (or make available) health and wellness programs.
11. Develop/select, implement and evaluate security plans to protect the company from liability.
12. Develop/select, implement and evaluate security plans to protect employees (for example, injuries resulting from workplace violence).
13. Develop/select, implement and evaluate incident and emergency response plans (for example, natural disasters, workplace safety threats, evacuation).

Knowledge:
52. Federal, state and local workplace health and safety laws and regulations (for example, OSHA, Drug-Free Workplace Act, ADA).
53. Workplace injury and occupational illness compensation laws and programs (for example, workers' compensation).
54. Investigation procedures of workplace safety, health and security enforcement agencies (for example, OSHA).
55. Workplace safety risks.
56. Workplace security risks (for example, theft, corporate espionage, information systems/technology and vandalism).
57. Potential violent behavior and workplace violence conditions.
58. General health and safety practices (for example, fire evacuation, HAZCOM, ergonomic evaluations).
59. Incident and emergency response plans.
60. Internal investigation and surveillance techniques.
61. Employee assistance programs.
62. Employee wellness programs.
63. Issues related to chemical use and dependency (for example, identification of symptoms, drug testing, discipline).

Core Knowledge Required by HR Professionals
64. Needs assessment and analysis.
65. Third-party contract management, including development of requests for proposals (RFPs).
66. Communication strategies.

67. Documentation requirements.
68. Adult learning processes.
69. Motivation concepts and applications.
70. Training methods.
71. Leadership concepts and applications.
72. Project management concepts and applications.
73. Diversity concepts and applications.
74. Human relations concepts and applications (for example, interpersonal and organizational behavior).
75. HR ethics and professional standards.
76. Technology and human resource information systems (HRIS) to support HR activities.
77. Qualitative and quantitative methods and tools for analysis, interpretation and decision-making purposes.
78. Change management.
79. Liability and risk management.
80. Job analysis and job description methods.
81. Employee records management (for example, retention, disposal).
82. The interrelationships among HR activities and programs across functional areas.

Resources

These selected resources, categorized by functional areas, may help you prepare for the PHR or SPHR exam. This is not an inclusive list of resources, but represents a solid foundation for a human resource professional library.

Strategic Management

Becker, Brian E., Huselid, Mark A., and Ulrich, David, *The HR Scorecard: Linking People, Strategy and Performance*, Harvard Business School Press, 2001.

Cascio, Wayne F., *Costing Human Resources: The Financial Impact of Behavior in Organizations*, Southwestern Publishing Company, 1999.

Cascio, Wayne F., *Managing Human Resources*, 6th ed., McGraw-Hill Companies, 2001.

DeCenzo, David A. and Robbins, Stephen P., *Human Resource Management*, 7th ed., John Wiley & Sons, 2001.

Dessler, Gary, *Human Resource Management*, 9th ed., Prentice-Hall, 2002.

Fitz-Enz, Jac, *How to Measure Human Resources Management*, McGraw-Hill, 2002.

Goldsmith, Marshall, Effron, Marc, and Gandossy, Robert, *Human Resources in the 21st Century*, John Wiley & Sons, 2003.

Greer, Charles R., *Strategic Human Resource Management*, Prentice Hall, 2000.

International HR Learning System, Society for Human Resource Management, 2002.

Lawler, Edward E., *Creating a Strategic Human Resource Organization: An Assessment of Trends and New Directions*, Stanford University Press, 2003.

Mathis, Robert L., *Human Resource Management with West Group Product Booklet*, 10th ed., South-Western College Publications, 2002.

Repa, Barbara Kate and Steingold, Fred S., *The Employer's Legal Handbook*, Nolo Press, 2003.

SHRM Learning System, Society for Human Resource Management, 2002.

Workforce Planning and Employment

Alhrichs, Nancy S., *Competing for Talent: Key Recruitment and Retention Strategies for Becoming an Employer of Choice*, Consulting Psychologists Press, 2000.

Arthur, Dian, *Employee Recruitment & Retention*, AMACOM, 2001.

Fitz-Enz, Jac, *The ROI of Human Capital: Measuring the Economic Value of Employee Performance*, AMACOM, 2000.

Human Resource Development

Phillips, Jack J. and Connell, Adele O., *Managing Employee Retention: A Strategic Accountability Approach*, Butterworth-Heineman/SHRM, 2003.

Lawler, Edward, *Rewarding Excellence*, Jossey-Bass, Inc., 2000.

Compensation and Benefits

Henderson, Richard I., *Compensation Management in a Knowledge-Based World*, 9th ed., Prentice-Hall, 2002.

Heneman, Robert L., *Business-Driven Compensation Policies: Integrating Compensation Systems with Corporate Strategies*, AMACOM, 2000.

Employee and Labor Relations

BNA Editorial Staff, *Grievance Guide*, 10th ed., BNA Books, 2000.

Carrell, Michael and Heavrin, Christina, *Labor Relations and Collective Bargaining Cases, Practices and Law*, Prentice Hall, 2000.

Occupational Health, Safety and Security

Milam-Perez, Lisa A., *HR How-To: Workplace Safety*, CCH, 2003.

Buckley, John F. and Green, Ronald M., *2003 State by State Guide to Workplace Safety Regulation*, Aspen Publishers, 2002.

PHR and SPHR Certification Exams

The Institute's PHR and SPHR certification exams are offered by computer in more than 250 Thomson Prometric testing centers during two eight-week windows. Both exams consist of 225 multiple-choice questions, each with four possible answers. Of the 225 questions, 25 are pretest questions not counted in the scoring of the exam but used for statistical purposes. Four hours are allotted to complete the exam. A passing (or cut) score is determined using the expert judgments of a standards setting panel. This score will vary depending on the actual exam form used.

The exams measure mastery of the domestic HR body of knowledge. Both exams cover the same functional areas but differ in terms of the individual test items and the functional area's percentage weightings. Preparation for the exam is best accomplished by mastering the application of the domestic HR body of knowledge.

HRCI uses multiple-choice exams because they:
- Are flexible and adaptable.
- Tend to be more reliable than other formats.
- Can accommodate a wide range of skills, knowledge and abilities to be measured.
- Provide a good sampling.
- Have low chance scores.
- Can be machine scored.

Multiple-choice items consist of three parts:

1. STEM: The stem states the problem or question to be answered.
2. CORRECT ANSWER: The correct answer is one of four potential options that represent the only correct response or best correct response. "Best" means a panel of experts would agree to this judgment.
3. DISTRACTORS: The remaining options are distractors and are incorrect responses. They are plausible, yet wrong or not the best possible answer.

The following is an example of the parts of a multiple-choice item:

Stem: Typically, the most unreliable tool utilized in the selection process is a(n):

Correct Answer: A. employment interview.

Distractor: B. selection test.

Distractor: C. physical exam.

Distractor: D. background check.

Certified HR professionals write all exam questions. These important volunteers serve on one of two HRCI Item Writing Panels and are given extensive training and specific guidelines on item development.

Exam questions (or items) go through an exhaustive item review process. A separate group of certified HR professionals (Item Review Panels) thoroughly scrutinize each item and perform a number of validity checks. Each remaining item is then categorized as either a PHR or SPHR item and coded to the Institute's test specifications.

A third group of HR professionals—the Exam Review Panel—reviews and approves each exam form before use.

This three-step process of item development, item review and exam review assures that items are:

- Clear, unambiguous and grammatically proper.
- Technically correct.
- Appropriate in terms of fairness—geographically, ethnically or culturally.
- Important for HR professionals to know.
- Correctly coded to the HRCI content outline.

The PHR and SPHR exams differ significantly in terms of the weights assigned to each of the functional areas. Of equal importance is the difference in focus and format of the individual questions on the exams. In general, PHR questions are more technical application questions. Many are at the operational level. On the other hand, SPHR questions tend to be more policy application questions. Many are at the strategic level. Additionally, there are a greater proportion of scenario questions on the SPHR exam. A scenario question poses an HR situation followed by a series of questions based on the information supplied. Scenario questions are particularly well suited to SPHR examinees because they represent typical situations that senior-level HR practitioners encounter and the diverse knowledge requirements needed to solve those situations.

The exams are administered through a professional testing service. This organization supplies expert counsel in exam design, construction and administration and also provides analysis of exam results.

Exam Preparation Methods, Strategies and Resources

Exam preparation is an important issue for candidates. There are a number of study methods available for the exams; selecting a method is a matter of individual preference based on what best fits into one's life and learning style. Methods range from the highly informal individual self-study to highly structured courses and workshops.

The strategy to prepare for the PHR or SPHR exam is equally important. Just like world-class athletes must peak at the precise moment of competition, so must candidates on exam day. In addition to being able to master the domestic HR body of knowledge, candidates should be both mentally and physically prepared to take the exam. Strategy is a critical element of preparation.

Study resources are also critical elements of preparation. Sometimes the resources will be a function of the preparation method selected. Other times, candidates will have to choose resources from a wide range of possibilities. A mistake in selecting resources can significantly affect test scores.

Choose a study method carefully. Because the exams measure mastery of the application of the domestic HR body of knowledge, it is impossible to train or teach to them. Instead, knowing the HR knowledge requirements and how to apply them are the best preparation. Study methods based on the actual exams' format are preferable because they familiarize test takers with the Institute's test specifications.

HRCI is a standard-setting and credentialing organization. As such, it does not provide professional development activities or endorse any particular study method. The Society for Human Resource Management's professional development department, however, may be a resource in surveying and selecting a preparation method.

Exam Preparation Methods

Self-Study

Self-study can either be individual, where candidates study at their own pace and on their own schedules, or it can be a group experience where there are regular meetings, mutual assistance and lively exchanges of ideas and information among members. The key concept to self-study programs, whether individual or group-based, is flexibility.

Individual self-study requires a high degree of personal discipline. Candidates who choose this method must develop study strategies, prepare schedules, and be committed to abide by those schedules. Prepackaged preparation systems such as the SHRM® Learning System are convenient for this purpose. Also, any of the general HR references cited in this book can be used as a starting point for individual self-study.

A modified version of individual self-study is paired self-study. This method uses the buddy system, where two candidates pair together and use the same format as with individual self-study. It is highly flexible, yet at the same time gives candidates a support system.

Group Study

Group study offers some advantages over individual and paired self-study. The camaraderie and group support can be a great asset. Many SHRM chapters sponsor certification study groups.

Key concepts to consider when forming a study group:
- Establish convenient meeting locations and times.
- Secure a certified HR professional to serve as a mentor to the group.
- Use pre- and posttests using an exam similar to the one used in this guide.
- Design a study format with a schedule and individual member assignments.
- Use multiple resources for preparation.

When flexibility is important, self-study methods, whether individual, paired, or group are potential ways to study for the exam.

College and University Courses

Many colleges and universities offer study courses to prepare for the exams. Most often these courses are offered on a noncredit/continuing education basis; some academic institutions, however, grant credit for these courses.

A number of colleges and universities have partnered with SHRM to offer a certification preparation course using the SHRM® Learning System, a study program that was developed using HRCI test specifications as a blueprint. Other colleges and universities use other materials.

Quality of instruction and resources should be carefully scrutinized, and it is always advisable to check references with past course participants before registering for such courses.

SHRM Chapter-Sponsored Short Courses

Many local SHRM chapters offer short courses to study for the PHR and SPHR exams. These short courses provide instruction and a structured program that cover the PHR and SPHR test specifications. Local SHRM chapters should be contacted to determine availability of these courses in your area (for a list of SHRM chapters, visit the SHRM Web site at www.shrm.org/chapters).

SHRM Certification Preparation Courses

Candidates with a good understanding of the HR field may be interested in the SHRM Review Course for Certification. This course is an intensive refresher or review of the domestic HR body of knowledge and is designed for experienced HR practitioners who need a refresher before the exam. It is offered nationally in selected locations before each of HRCI's exam windows. Information about this course can be obtained by calling the SHRM professional development department at (800) 283-7476 or by visiting the SHRM Web site at www.shrm.org.

Private Training Organizations

Some private training organizations now offer courses to prepare for the HRCI exams. Candidates should be sure that the approach used in the course corresponds to the PHR and SPHR test specifications.

If the certification method employs instructors, it is important that they be certified. It is hard—if not impossible—to teach about an exam one has not taken. Personal experiences of instructors offer valuable insights and increase the comfort levels of examinees.

Regardless of the method, a high degree of personal commitment is needed to receive the most benefit from the preparation experience.

Strategies

Any preparation method must have a strategy to maximize self-assessment, structure time, build mental and physical preparedness and address post-exam emotions.

Self-Assessment

No two candidates bring the same education, experience and preparation to the table. As a result, it is important to conduct an honest self-assessment of your qualifications and HR work experience.

Begin by reviewing your education and work experience in light of the test specifications. Compare your resume with the test specifications. In what areas have education and experience given you a strong knowledge and application base? What will you have to work on? Make a list of your strengths and weaknesses.

Next, answer the sample test questions in this book, resisting the temptation to look at the answers before completing the test. Correct the test and total your score in each of the functional areas of the exam. Is there a correlation between the test results and the self-assessment? Keep in mind that there are only 125 sample test questions; there are 200 scoreable questions in the actual exam.

HRCI also offers candidates an online assessment exam at www.hrci.org. This exam will help you determine your strengths and weaknesses in each of the functional areas of the exam and allows you to become familiar with the format and difficulty level of the exam questions. You may take both a PHR and SPHR assessment exam. Both are excellent indicators of preparedness for the actual exam. More information about the assessment exam can be found on page 6.

These kinds of self-assessments will help candidates center on those areas where the most preparation is needed. Always focus on the areas where you need the most preparation based upon the weightings of the specific exam (PHR or SPHR) you will take.

Structuring Time

Once the self-assessment is completed, map a formal approach in how you will spend your time studying for the test. Structuring time will be different depending on the level of exam (PHR or SPHR) and the self-assessment. The following are sample eight-, 10- and 12-week study schedules:

Eight-Week Schedule

PHR Exam		SPHR Exam	
Week	**Topic**	**Week**	**Topic**
1	Introduction and Pretest	1	Introduction and Pretest
2	Strategic Management	2	Strategic Management
3	Workforce Planning and Employment	3	Strategic Management
4	Human Resource Development	4	Workforce Planning and Employment
5	Compensation and Benefits	5	Human Resource Development
6	Compensation and Benefits; Employee and Labor Relations	6	Compensation and Benefits
7	Employee and Labor Relations	7	Employee and Labor Relations
8	Occupational Health, Safety and Security; Posttest	8	Occupational Health, Safety and Security; Posttest

Ten-Week Schedule

PHR Exam		SPHR Exam	
Week	**Topic**	**Week**	**Topic**
1	Introduction and Pretest	1	Introduction and Pretest
2	Strategic Management	2	Strategic Management
3	Workforce Planning and Employment	3	Strategic Management
4	Workforce Planning and Employment	4	Workforce Planning and Employment
5	Human Resource Development	5	Workforce Planning and Employment; Human Resource Development
6	Compensation and Benefits	6	Human Resource Development; Compensation and Benefits
7	Compensation and Benefits	7	Compensation and Benefits
8	Employee and Labor Relations	8	Employee and Labor Relations
9	Employee and Labor Relations	9	Employee and Labor Relations
10	Occupational Health, Safety and Security; Posttest	10	Occupational Health, Safety and Security; Posttest

Twelve-Week Schedule

PHR Exam		SPHR Exam	
Week	**Topic**	**Week**	**Topic**
1	Introduction and Pretest	1	Introduction and Pretest
2	Strategic Management	2	Strategic Management
3	Strategic Management	3	Strategic Management
4	Workforce Planning and Placement	4	Strategic Management
5	Workforce Planning and Placement	5	Workforce Planning and Placement
6	Workforce Planning and Placement; Human Resource Development	6	Workforce Planning and Placement
7	Human Resource Development	7	Human Resource Development
8	Compensation and Benefits	8	Compensation and Benefits
9	Compensation and Benefits	9	Compensation and Benefits
10	Employee and Labor Relations	10	Employee and Labor Relations
11	Employee and Labor Relations	11	Employee and Labor Relations
12	Occupational Health, Safety and Security; Posttest	12	Occupational Health, Safety and Security; Posttest

Mental and Physical Preparedness

Cramming the week or night before the exam is a common mistake made by many candidates. In reality, such behavior hurts exam performance. Preparation is best if spaced over an extended period of time.

Given the nature of exams, a clear head will help performance more than any limited knowledge gained by last-minute cramming. HRCI exams are intellectually challenging and fatiguing; arriving at a test site already tired from cramming the night before is not a wise strategy. Prepare early and relax the night before the exam. Go out to eat or to a movie the night before, get a good night's rest, and come to the testing center relaxed and alert.

Post-Exam Emotions

It is important to acknowledge and prepare for post-exam emotions. The two emotions that are most likely to occur after taking the test are both frustration-related. First, candidates report feeling frustrated because they do not know how they performed on the exam. Second, they feel frustrated because they do not know what they could have done to perform any better. Both of these emotions are quite common for any exam that assesses mastery in a particular field.

Unlike curriculum-based tests, these exams cannot be "taught to." Realize that these feelings of frustration are common, recognize them and be prepared to address them after the exam.

Resources

Some preparation methods, such as university or college courses, will provide or identify the resources to be used in the class. Other preparation methods leave it up to the candidate. Therefore, choosing the appropriate resources is critically important.

Because the exams measure mastery of the entire domestic HR body of knowledge, there is no one best resource to use to study for the exam.

To understand the importance of using a variety of resources, imagine a giant globe filled with marbles. Each marble represents one piece of the domestic HR body of knowledge from each of the functional areas. Each level of the exam is composed of a random drawing of marbles according to the percentage listed for each functional area in the test specifications.

If you can visualize the giant globe filled with thousands of marbles, you can easily see that it is impossible to predict which of the marbles will be on the exam. It is equally impossible for any one preparatory resource to contain all the marbles. This is why HRCI recommends using a variety of resources for the most comprehensive exposure to the test specifications.

The Institute's mission is to identify the domestic HR body of knowledge and to develop test specifications that measure mastery of this knowledge. It does not develop the resources to teach the test specifications to candidates. To maintain exam integrity, HRCI separates itself from the development of preparatory resources and does not endorse any particular resource. The following, however, is a partial list of available resources. For a more complete list of resources, please refer to the resources in Section III of this guide.

The SHRM® Learning System covers all functional areas of the test specifications and includes self-directed modules, application activities and end-of-module exams. It was designed to follow the HRCI test specifications and is available from SHRM.

HR textbooks are also a good resource. Be sure to select textbooks that are up-to-date, since the HR field changes rapidly. Textbooks published more than one or two years ago should be used with great caution. It is also recommended that several texts be used, rather than just one, so that candidates see different perspectives.

Custom-designed resources are used by some SHRM chapters and proprietary companies. Many of these resources are not original works but are committee-assembled compilations of other resources.

Lending libraries are popular with some SHRM chapters. Learning resources are purchased and made available to chapter members at no cost or for a nominal fee. This allows members to review materials they may not otherwise be able to afford.

Test-Taking Skills

It is natural to have some anxieties and nervousness about taking an exam; the anxiety level is likely to be even greater for candidates who have been out of school for several years.

All of the questions on the PHR and SPHR exams are multiple-choice. The question statement is called the stem and the answers are called choices. Some choices are designed to be plausible but incorrect. These are called distractors.

Questions on the exam are of different types, especially at the PHR level. Some will be identification questions, which means that definitions of concepts or facts are being assessed. Relationship questions are used to test how one concept is related to or affects another one. Other questions are application in nature; a situation is posed and the choices reflect applying certain facts to the situation.

The following are some test-taking suggestions to help candidates perform up to their capabilities and knowledge:

- **Use the white erase board that will be provided at your testing station.** Feel free to make notes and simple calculations. You will be asked to return the white erase board with your completed exam.
- **Trust your first impression.** There is a correct answer to each question. It is widely believed that your first impression of the correct answer will be a better choice.
- **Avoid over-analyzing.** Be careful not to read too much into an answer.
- **If uncertain, mark the question and return to it later.** If you cannot decide on an answer, mark the question and return to it after answering all of the questions on the exam. It is possible that later questions may trigger information useful for those "undecided" questions.
- **Don't stop.** If you are stumped by a question, continue to the next one. Otherwise, you may lose valuable time. Mark the question and return to it later.

- **Don't look for answer patterns.** The psychometric testing process used by HRCI ensures that questions do not fall into patterns. Contrary to some myths, "C" is not necessarily the most frequent answer and the first answer may be correct.
- **The length of an answer is a false clue.** It is a myth that the longer an answer, the more likely it is to be correct. It often is more difficult to write incorrect distractors than the correct answer, so it is just as likely that the longest distractor is incorrect as it is correct.
- **Eliminate obvious distractors.** For most questions, there are two distractors that usually appear to be incorrect; one that is likely to be plausible but incorrect; and one correct answer. When you first read a question, you should be able to eliminate two of the answers as incorrect. If you cannot decide between the other two, move on to the next question and return to the unanswered question later.
- **Try to identify the answer before reading the choices.** After reading the question, try to answer the question before reading the choices. By doing this, you will more likely have one answer stand out as being correct.
- **Use "educated guesses."** If you still cannot decide on a correct answer after eliminating one or two choices, choose one anyway. There is no penalty for guessing on the exam.
- **Don't worry about what you don't know.** If you don't know the answer to a question, don't fret about it and let it affect your outlook when answering other questions.
- **Review your answers.** After going through all the questions on the exam, go back and answer the questions left unanswered the first time. Also, be sure that you answered all questions.
- **Don't rush.** There are no points for finishing first. Use the time allotted to review and check your answers. Keep in mind that someone who finishes early may know less than you do, so don't feel self-conscious about being among the last to complete the exam.
- **Don't worry after the test.** Many people feel drained and inadequate after taking a long exam. That feeling is not necessarily directly related to doing poorly on the exam.

Sample Test Questions

These sample questions are designed to familiarize candidates with the style and format of PHR and SPHR exam questions. This practice test is shorter than the actual exams (it has 125 practice items versus 200 scoreable questions on the actual exam). **None of these items will be found on the HRCI exams but are representative of the types of questions found in them.** To help you, a scoring sheet and the rationale for the answers follow these practice items. The answers include how the items are coded according to the HRCI content outline.

Remember to select the BEST answer. Good luck!

1. For which position would an employer most likely be able to support a BFOQ based upon sex?
   a. Sportscaster.
   — b. Locker room attendant.
   c. Nurse.
   d. OB-GYN physician.

2. Which of the following positions is considered an HR specialist?
   — a. Industrial Relations Director.
   b. Human Resource Manager.
   c. Personnel Administrator.
   d. Human Resource Team Leader.

3. In conducting a cost/benefit analysis of a training program, costs are often broken down into direct and indirect costs. Which of the following represents an indirect cost?
   a. Participants' salary.
   b. Training department's overhead.
   c. Training materials.
   d. Trainer's salary.

4. What restriction is placed on NLRB certification of a unit of security guards?
   a. The same restrictions as in units of other employees.
   b. The union seeking certification must represent only guards.
   c. The expiration date of the guards' contract cannot coincide with that of the plant union.
   d. The union must include all plant employees.

5. An expatriate's expenses for home travel are deductible for U.S. tax purposes if the trip is made to:
    a. the United States.
    b. the principal residence in the United States.
    c. anywhere outside of the country of assignment.
    d. the location of the last employment in the United States.

6. Which of the following is the best predictor of future performance?
    a. Past performance. ⌣
    b. Psychological tests.
    c. Present supervisor assessment.
    d. Former supervisor assessment.

7. Which type of data is generally unavailable to an HR manager in evaluating the effectiveness of an external employee assistance program?
    a. Initial diagnosis category.
    b. Referral source.
    c. Vitalization percent.
    d. Treatment outcome.

8. What is the most effective form of upward communication?
    a. Suggestion systems.
    b. Employee petitions.
    c. Grievance procedures.
    d. Direct discussions between supervisors and employees.

9. In which of the following content areas is it most difficult to evaluate the effectiveness of training?
    a. Typing skills.
    b. Human relations.
    c. Accident reduction.
    d. Grievance reduction.

10. Which of the following questions asked during an interview would most likely give rise to an inference of discrimination?
    a. Describe your military experience.
    b. Do you have a job-related disability?
    c. To what professional organizations do you belong?
    d. Describe the extracurricular activities you did in college.

11. In order for a union to prevail during a representation election, it must win:
    a. a majority of the votes cast in an election.
    b. 51% of the votes of those eligible to vote in the election.
    c. two-thirds of the votes cast in the election.
    d. 30% of the votes cast.

12. When conducting an environmental scan, supply and demand for specific skills, changes in competitors' practices, and unemployment levels are all examples of which of the following influences?
    a. Geographic.
    b. Governmental.
    — c. Labor market.
    d. Union.

13. To ensure that a job-training program is valid, a trainer will emphasize:
    a. conducting a job/task analysis.
    b. observing and interviewing the most productive incumbents in a job.
    c. surveying what programs are commercially available in the specific job area.
    d. outlining the traits necessary to perform the job.

14. How do employees tend to perceive the pay of their peers and supervisors when they do not know what the actual pay is?
    a. They overestimate the pay of both their peers and their supervisors.
    b. They underestimate the pay of both their peers and their supervisors.
    — c. They underestimate the pay of their peers and overestimate that of their supervisors.
    d. They overestimate the pay of their peers and underestimate that of their supervisors.

15. At the beginning of a given year, a shipping department has four people, each paid $1,000 per month. In that year, each of these employees receives a pay raise of $100 per month. The raises are given January 1, March 1, July 1 and November 1, respectively. The salary increases increase the payroll cost for the year by:
    a. 6.25%.
    b. 7%.
    — c. 9%.
    d. 10%.

16. In order to avoid a charge of negligent hiring, an employer should give special attention to which phase of a selection system?
    a. Interviewing.
    b. Honesty testing.
    ~ c. Reference checking.
    d. Medical exams.

17. All employers with _____ or more employees, must file an annual EEO-I (or I-VI) with the EEOC.
    ✓ a. 15.
    b. 20.
    c. 50.
    d. 100.

18. The most difficult problem in forecasting demand for employees is:
    a. forecasting internal supply.
    ✓ b. estimating turnover patterns.
    c. determining the supply of human resources.
    d. determining the relationship between personnel demand and the firm's output.

19. In order to prevail in a charge of discrimination based upon selecting participants for a training program, it is most appropriate for the organization to:
    a. establish a quota system to ensure minority representation.
    ~ b. ensure the selection of trainees is well documented and does not result in adverse impact.
    c. utilize a self-nomination method of selecting participants.
    d. use diversity training as the initial phase of the training program.

20. The proportion of a sales representative's income that is incentive pay should be relatively large when:
    a. the company does not do much advertising.
    ~ b. customer service is a major consideration.
    c. the product is superior to its competition.
    d. the nature of the product requires team selling.

21. Which of the following is the best process for validating an employment application form as a selection device?
    - a. Correlating responses to test scores.
    - b. Determining if the information reported on the application is correct.
    - c. Examining each item and determining to what extent it helped to predict job success.
    - d. Receiving approval from top management for its use in selection of applicants.

22. The primary advantage of a computerized internal skills inventory is that:
    - a. it permits employers to predict which additional skills are needed for the workforce of the future.
    - b. managers have access to much more sensitive information than in manual systems.
    - c. EEOC guidelines recommend automated systems.
    - d. job candidates have more confidence in systems that minimize the possibility of personal bias.

23. Which type of psychological test measures an individual's overall ability to learn?
    - a. Aptitude.
    - b. Interest.
    - c. Personality.
    - d. Specific abilities.

24. Which of the following may legally be stated in an organization's employee relations policy?
    - a. Increase pay for remaining nonunion.
    - b. Plant closure if unionized.
    - c. Organizational opposition to unions.
    - d. Endorsement of a specific union.

25. What is the primary purpose of a flexible benefit plan?
    - a. Allow employees to contribute pretax dollars to buy additional benefits.
    - b. Continuously update benefit options as employees' needs and desires change.
    - c. Pass along benefit premium increases to employees.
    - d. Combine all time-off benefits into a pool from which an employee can take off with pay.

26. For effective learning to occur, the amount of information, its complexity and its rate of presentation should be directed to:
    a. fall within perceptual and comprehension spans of the learners.
    ➝ b. accommodate the organizational culture in which the learners exist.
    c. fall within the levels with which the instructors teaching the material are comfortable.
    d. accommodate post-training practices felt most desirable by employee's line management.

27. Assuming no willful violation, what is the statute of limitations for recovery of back pay under the Fair Labor Standards Act?
    a. 2 years.
    b. 3 years.
    c. 4 years.
    d. 5 years.

28. During a unionization drive, which of the following may a supervisor legally do?
    a. Visit the homes of employees for the purpose of urging them to reject the union.
    ‒ b. Inform the employees that he or she believes the international union may attempt to control the local membership.
    c. Make speeches to massed assemblies of employees on company time within a 24-hour period of time before the election.
    d. Speak to employees one on one in the office of the management official and urge them to vote against the union.

29. The first step in establishing an HRIS is to:
    a. develop the database.
    ➝ b. determine the information needs.
    c. establish a security and control system.
    d. select between PC and mainframe applications.

30. Underutilization is defined as having fewer minorities or women in a job classification than would be expected based on:
    a. the area population.
    ➝ b. their availability in the reasonable recruitment area.
    c. their overall representation in the facility workforce.
    d. the availability of required skills in the regional labor market.

31. Which of the following would be a recommended compensation practice for a startup business that wishes to create an innovative, entrepreneurial culture?

   a. Offer incentive bonuses and stock ownership plans.

   b. Establish high starting pay rates to attract the most talented employees.

   c. Offer a benefits program that exceeds competitors.

   d. Establish step or longevity-based pay increases.

32. In a matrix organizational structure:

   a. employees have three or more supervisors.

   b. two organizational structures exist at the same time.

   c. productivity is enhanced because of strict functional accountability.

   d. line authority is strengthened.

33. Which of the following generally represents the greatest cost factor for training provided to employees by their organization?

   a. Space material expenses.

   b. Program developer salary cost.

   c. Trainee hours lost from production.

   d. Consulting fees and equipment costs.

34. A supervisor who has an employee with a suspected alcohol problem impacting performance should:

   a. confront the employee immediately about the alcohol problem.

   b. diagnose the employee's problem before trying to counsel him or her.

   c. document the situation before discussing the decreased performance with the employee.

   d. never expect the employee to return to his or her previous performance level.

35. Which of the following statements best describes diversity programs?

   a. Lawful reverse discrimination.

   b. Valuing differences.

   c. Assimilating differences.

   d. Required for government contractors.

36. In order for a position to qualify under the executive exemption to the Fair Labor Standards Act, the position must:
    a. be considered an officer of the organization.
    b. have a bachelor's degree or higher.
    c. direct the work of at least two other full-time employees.
    d. spend less than 30% of the time on nonexempt duties.

37. What kind of arbitrator is selected by the parties to serve on a single grievance case?
    a. An ad hoc arbitrator.
    b. An interest arbitrator.
    c. A permanent umpire.
    d. A tri-partite arbitrator.

38. If a group is highly cohesive, the individuals in the group are more likely to:
    a. play devil's advocate with each other.
    b. value group norms and goals.
    c. exhibit dysfunctional competition with group members.
    d. desire a strong automatic leadership style.

39. Contributory pension plans:
    a. require contributions by the employee who will benefit from the income upon retirement.
    b. are funded solely by employer contributions.
    c. must be funded by contributions by the employer from current income.
    d. prohibit employees from participating in another retirement plan simultaneously.

40. For virtual jobs performed by individuals shifting from project to project or working on cross-functional teams that change frequently, a job analysis must focus on the:
    a. competencies required and how they are assessed and maintained.
    b. knowledge, skills and abilities needed to perform the jobs.
    c. tasks, duties and responsibilities of the virtual employees.
    d. essential job functions needed for the changing jobs.

41. Adults learn BEST when the material to be taught is:

    a. standardized.

    — b. integrated with their experience.

    c. presented in a classroom lecture format.

    d. geared to the level that is slightly more difficult than they can easily handle.

42. Which of the following is an independent contractor?

    a. A temporary programmer who works part time in the data processing department for $9 an hour.

    — b. An auditor who performs a two-week audit of the company's financial records each year.

    c. A salesperson who has an office in his or her home and reports to a national sales manager.

    d. An executive who has an employment contract with a company regarding change of control.

43. Major changes to supporting cultures in mature organizations should occur:

    — a. regularly once every five years to keep pace with competitors.

    b. with each new yearly business cycle.

    c. infrequently, no more than once every seven to 10 years.

    d. rarely, only once or twice during the organization's life cycle in order to minimize the negative effects of change.

44. A data entry person earned $8.00 per hour plus a weekly attendance incentive of $20.00. If the employee works 42 hours in a workweek, how much total compensation should be paid?

    a. $356.50

    b. $364.48

    c. $365.50

    d. $372.48

45. How could the heavy use of employee referrals for job vacancies violate nondiscrimination laws?
    a. By minority employees refusing to refer job applicants.
    b. Where it results in an undesirable status quo of an underrepresented workforce.
    c. Where minority employees constitute the majority of employees in the workforce.
    d. Where an Affirmative Action plan is not required to correct an imbalance.

46. If a candidate is recruited and hired through two professional employment agency contacts and both agencies claim the fee for the referral, what is the best approach to settling the claims?
    a. Pay the fee at 50 percent of each agency since both made the referral.
    b. Pay the full fee to each agency, since both agencies referred the candidate.
    c. Recommend the two agencies negotiate the fee, since only one fee is to be paid.
    d. Examine the referral documents as to dates referred and pay the fee to the agency whose referral was received first.

47. If the union asks the employer for use of company vehicles when not needed for work to transport their members to a union picnic, what is the proper response?
    a. Decline the request.
    b. Offer the use at a standard market price.
    c. Offer the use for a charge of gas and oil.
    d. Offer the use for a nominal fee.

48. Which action could improve the effectiveness of assessment centers in selecting employees from within the firm for higher-level positions?
    a. Self-nomination.
    b. Greater emphasis on interpersonal skills.
    c. Greater use of staff T&D people.
    d. Minimal participation by line managers.

49. What is a draw, as used for sales representatives?
    a. Money that is to be used to pay for traveling expenses.
    b. Money that is paid on a regular basis in addition to commissions.
    c. Money that is paid on a regular basis but that must be earned from commissions or paid back.
    d. Money that is paid on a regular basis to be applied against commissions but not paid back if unearned.

50. The HR control process is normally thought of as containing the following steps: I.) comparing actual with expected performance; II.) observing and measuring performance; III.) setting expectations or standards; and IV.) taking corrective action. What is the proper sequence of these steps?
    a. I, II, III, IV.
    b. II, I, IV, III.
    c. IV, II, III, I.
    d. III, II, I, IV.

51. If an HR practitioner developed an economic or statistical model to identify costs and benefits associated with an HR program, this would be called a(n):
    a. HR audit.
    b. human resource accounting.
    c. break-even analysis.
    d. utility analysis.

52. Simulation and gaming training is most often directed toward improvements in:
    a. decision-making.
    b. human relation problem solving.
    c. diversity initiatives.
    d. culture.

53. The most accepted method of calculating turnover rate is to compute for a given period the:
    a. ratio of new hires to total workforce.
    b. ratio of separations to total workforce.
    c. ratio of people who quit to new hires.
    d. number of separations in a particular department or unit.

54. For many years, employees at a certain company took two daily 10-minute coffee breaks. After being organized, the company received a request for two 15-minute coffee breaks. The company should:
   a. discontinue its practice.
   b. continue its practice and negotiate.
   c. discontinue its practice and negotiate.
   d. continue the practice but refuse to negotiate.

55. Which of the following is NOT included in a party-in-interest as defined by ERISA?
   a. Employee with less than one year of service.
   b. Owner of at least 50% of the property of the employer.
   c. Trustees, custodians and persons providing services to such a plan.
   d. Administrators, fiduciaries and trustees of an employee benefit plan.

56. Which of the following concerning benefits is of strategic importance and should be addressed by an organization?
   a. The cost of FMLA leave and other required leave.
   b. The mix between indirect and direct compensation.
   c. The tax consequences for employees of the benefits.
   d. The provision of government mandated benefits.

57. An organization that desires to use a job analysis method that allows for a quick response rate and gathering of data on a large number of jobs, should use which method of job analysis?
   a. Observation.
   b. Interview.
   c. Questionnaire.
   d. Functional Job Analysis.

58. An HR audit is a(n):
   a. attempt to quantify the value of its human resources to the organization.
   b. aggregate skills inventory of the organization's human resources.
   c. formal research effort to evaluate the current state of human resource management within the organization.
   d. part of a human resource accounting system.

59. What is one of the most frequently encountered practical challenges associated with the use of case studies?
 ☞ a. There are no final or absolute solutions in case studies.
 b. They are relatively unavailable in package form in the training marketplace.
 c. The instructor must select a case with which the training group can identify.
 d. Trainees are overzealous in wanting to apply their case solutions to real life.

60. Good-faith bargaining requires that both labor and management:
 a. reach agreement on the mandatory items under negotiation.
 b. meet and discuss those mandatory items brought up by the other side.
 c. fairly represent themselves by not making inflammatory statements about the other side.
 d. reach agreement on all mandatory and permissive items brought up by the other side.

61. Which of the following methods of organizational development has been criticized for the emotional stress it creates for some participants?
 a. Team building.
 b. Transactional analysis.
 c. Sensitivity training.
 d. Survey feedback.

62. For which of the following types of employees are maturity curves most used as a basis of compensation?
 a. Executives.
 b. Management trainees.
 c. Professional personnel.
 d. Long service nonexempt employees.

63. To measure total organizational hiring costs, which of the following is most appropriate to consider?
 a. Only budgeted expenditures.
 b. Direct out-of-pocket expenditures.
 c. Both indirect and direct costs.
 d. Cost data supplied by the Department of Labor.

64. Employers under the OSHA Bloodborne Pathogens standard must:
    a. provide free hepatitis B vaccinations to all employees.
    b. establish a written exposure control plan.
    c. communicate an employee's bloodborne infection status to co-workers upon request.
    d. conduct regular blood tests on all employees.

65. The Worker Adjustment and Retraining Notification Act (WARN) of 1988 requires:
    a. severance pay to workers who lose their jobs permanently.
    b. sixty days notice if a mass layoff or facility closing is to occur.
    c. full disclosure regarding reasons for plant closing.
    d. a re-education allowance to workers over age 60.

66. Which of the following constitutes an intrinsic reward?
    a. Pay.
    b. Working conditions.
    c. The job itself.
    d. Complimentary supervision.

67. In order to reduce information overload, orientation programs should:
    a. be modularized and spread out over a period of time.
    b. be conducted only after an employee has served on the job for a specified period of time.
    c. include a detailed employee reference manual for later use.
    d. provide continuous feedback to participants.

68. The primary test to determine the reasonableness of a work rule is whether or not the:
    a. union has requested a change in the rule or its elimination.
    b. rule furthers a strict disciplinary approach to managing the workforce.
    c. employees agree that the rule is necessary if the plant is to operate efficiently.
    d. rule is reasonably related to a legitimate business reason.

69. One advantage of having an executive search firm on retainer is that:
    a. search firms are ethically bound not to approach employees of client companies in their search efforts for another client.
    b. it establishes an ongoing professional relationship that enables positions to be filled more efficiently.
    c. search firms give their clients first refusal of an outstanding candidate.
    d. in the long run, they are less expensive.

70. During negotiations the union and company were discussing wage increases for production operators. The company claimed that granting a wage increase would give the operators more money than the supervisors were making. The union requested the salary schedules for supervisors. What is the company required to do?
    a. Refuse the request.
    b. Provide the supervisors' salary schedule to the union.
    c. Refuse the request, but give the information to a mediator.
    d. Ignore the request.

71. Which of the following is not used as a method to segment a relevant labor market?
    a. Geographic.
    b. Type of skill.
    c. Income level.
    d. Industry.

72. In training supervisors for handling discipline and discharge incidents, which of the following is the most appropriate training method?
    a. On the job.
    b. Case study.
    c. Programmed instruction.
    d. Role-play.

73. What is the most important requirement for a qualified benefit plan in order to be eligible for favorable tax status?
    a. The plan must integrate with Social Security.
    b. The plan must not discriminate in favor of highly compensated executives.
    c. The plan must shift income to post-working retirement years.
    d. The plan must provide some type of retirement annuity.

74. A weighted application form is most appropriate for which type of position?
    a. Top-level executive positions.
    b. Multiple incumbent positions.
    c. Positions that have underutilization of minorities.
    d. Unskilled positions.

75. An employee reports to work one morning with a weird hairstyle in order to impress the supervisor. The supervisor ignores this new hairstyle with the expectation that it will not be repeated. What type of behavior modification strategy was employed?
    a. Extinction.
    b. Punishment.
    c. Negative reinforcement.
    d. Positive reinforcement.

76. If many people perform a similar set of tasks, what would be the preferred method of collecting information for assessing training needs?
    a. Job inventory questionnaire.
    b. Employee opinion.
    c. Observation and interview.
    d. Performance appraisal data.

77. A manager summons a unionized employee to the manager's office to be interviewed about a work rule violation. The employee demands a union representative be present. Which of the following responses should the manager give?
    a. The meeting will be conducted without the union representative present, because it is management's right to discipline.
    b. No grievance has been filed so there is no entitlement to union representation.
    c. A union representative is only permitted if the contract provides for union representation at discipline meetings.
    d. A union representative may be present for investigative meetings that lead to discipline if requested by the employee.

78. According to workers' compensation law, payment of compensation is made to an employee for any injury:
   a. without regard to who is at fault.
   b. only when it is due to the employer's negligence.
   c. except one due to the employee's carelessness.
   d. except for one due to the negligence of a co-worker.

79. As a holiday absence control practice, employers commonly:
   a. require employees to work the day before and after a holiday to be eligible for holiday pay.
   b. provide employees flexibility as to holidays they want off.
   c. pay time and one-half to hourly employees who work the holiday in lieu of holiday pay.
   d. require employees to use vacation days if they don't work on a holiday.

80. If an HR manager notices the posting of a number of pinups—foldouts of scantily clothed females—out on the shop floor, the HR manager should have the posters removed based upon which theory of sexual harassment?
   a. Employment consequence.
   b. Employment conditions.
   c. Vicarious liability.
   d. Hostile environment.

81. Compensatory time off for nonexempt employees can be given in the private sector if:
   a. the hourly wage is at least one and one-half times the minimum wage.
   b. it is equivalent to the number of hours worked overtime within the same pay period.
   c. it is used within the next three months by the employee.
   d. it is given at the rate of one and one-half times hours worked over a 40-hour week.

82. It is not discriminatory during pre-employment inquiries to ask about an applicant's record on:
   a. workers' compensation.
   b. driving.
   c. arrests.
   d. favoring unions.

83. A salary survey shows the following data:

Organization	Number Incumbents	Average Salary
A	15	$700
B	10	700
C	25	700
D	50	800

How does the weighted average salary compare to the unweighted average salary?

a. It is $50 lower.
b. It is $25 lower.
c. It is $25 higher.
d. It is $50 higher.

84. In a firm's training and development program, the trainee must believe that improved skills will lead to desired outcomes and that his or her effort in the training program will result in improved skills. These assumptions are related to which theory of motivation?

a. Expectancy theory.
b. Reinforcement theory.
c. Motivation-hygiene theory.
d. Equity theory.

85. Leadership research has identified two major leader behaviors; one of which focuses on people and interpersonal relationships. What is the focus of the other?

a. Power and authority.
b. Task accomplishment.
c. Organizational culture.
d. Profitability and financial accountability.

86. When significant aspects of performance are not measured by the appraisal form, this is called:

a. criterion contamination.
b. criterion deficiency.
c. rater bias error.
d. contrast error.

87. Which of the following constitutes a major function of the Federal Mediation and Conciliation Service?
   a. Representing employees under the National Labor Relations Act.
   b. Advising companies and unions regarding the handling of grievances.
   c. Helping companies and unions to reach agreement during contract negotiations.
   d. Representing employees who feel they have been discriminated against based on their civil rights.

88. An applicant who was previously fired for misconduct by another employer does not list that employment experience on the application form and is subsequently hired. One month later, this omission is discovered. How should this situation be handled?
   a. The incident should be overlooked and considered a casual omission.
   b. The employee should receive a written disciplinary letter over the incident.
   c. The employee should be fired for falsification of the application.
   d. The previous employer should be contacted to determine the cause of the prior dismissal.

89. What is the most important factor contributing to success of a TQM program in an organization?
   a. Organizational culture supports the TQM program.
   b. Union acceptance of the TQM program.
   c. Statistical aptitude of supervisors in quality control.
   d. Individual rather than group awards for performance.

90. ERISA imposes which of the following on compensation systems:
   a. funding requirements.
   b. competitive compensation rates.
   c. arbitration procedures.
   d. mandatory pension plans.

91. Which of the following subject areas receive greatest emphasis in organizational sales training programs aimed at experienced and inexperienced salespersons?
    a. Product knowledge.
    b. Marketing orientation.
    c. Selling techniques.
    d. Company orientation.

92. If a supervisor gives an employee a very high rating on "quality of work" and allows that rating to influence the rating on "quantity of work," the supervisor is guilty of:
    a. leniency error.
    b. central tendency error.
    c. rater bias error.
    d. halo/horned error.

93. In translating the results of a salary survey into actual wage rates, what statistical technique would be most appropriate to use?
    a. Least-squares method.
    b. Dispersion method.
    c. Correlation method.
    d. Expected variance method.

94. An employment interviewer says to a job applicant "...that experience sounds interesting...," after which he or she pauses, waiting for the applicant to elaborate further. What type of interview technique is being used?
    a. Behavioral.
    b. Stress Interview technique.
    c. Nondirective interviewing technique.
    d. Patterned interview.

95. Which of the following factors is not related to pay compression?
    a. Higher starting salaries dictated by increased market pressures.
    b. Unionized hourly pay increases that overtake supervisory and nonunion hourly rates.
    c. Merit increases that reward existing employees for higher productivity.
    d. Recruitment of new college graduates at pay levels above those of current job holders.

96. In performance appraisal systems, central tendency is the most common error found in using:
   a. essays.
   b. ranking.
   c. critical incidents.
   d. graphic rating scales.

97. Which of the following BEST describes the relationship between human resource planning and strategic organizational planning?
   a. Human resource planning is the essential component of strategic organizational planning.
   b. They are separate and distinct activities.
   c. Human resource planning must be completed before strategic organizational planning begins.
   d. Both types of planning are equivalent components of overall organizational planning.

98. Which of the following approaches will most effectively minimize employee-relations difficulties?
   a. Install a suggestion system.
   b. Increase the amount of supervision provided employees.
   c. Maintain an open line of direct and factual communication with employees.
   d. Implement a quality control program.

99. After implementing a new job evaluation plan, it is best to deal with red circle rates by:
   a. reducing their salary to the new maximum for their respective job grade.
   b. allowing their base rate to increase as all others do in the same job grade.
   c. reducing the salary to the minimum of the range and providing the employee the amount of the decrease in the form of a bonus.
   d. freezing their salary until job grade maximum increases to catch up with the red circle rate.

100. The use of an aptitude test in a selection program best predicts:
     a. skill level.
     b. job knowledge.
     c. manual dexterity.
     d. training performance.

101. Which of the following training methods would be most appropriate to use to help a new manager develop planning and conceptual skills?
     a. Sensitivity training.
     b. Human relations training.
     c. Simulation training.
     d. Role-play training.

102. Why are skill tests more accurate in predicting failures than successes?
     a. They assess "can do" rather than "will do."
     b. The scores are more reliable in lower ranges than higher ranges.
     c. If applicants fail a test there is no certainty they will be unsuccessful on the job.
     d. They are designed to eliminate potential failures rather than identify potential successes.

103. The total span of possible work hours in a flextime environment is referred to as:
     a. core time.
     b. bandwidth time.
     c. compressed work time.
     d. contingent time.

104. Multisource assessments (360-degree appraisals) are most relevant and useful for:
     a. retention decisions.
     b. developmental purposes.
     c. merit pay decisions.
     d. candidates for international assignments.

105. If a labor relations manager discovers that an above-average union employee who has been employed at the plant for nine years falsified an employment application by stating that he or she lost his or her previous job from layoff when, in fact, he or she was discharged, what should the manager do?
   a. Suspend the employee for 30 days.
   b. Schedule a grievance hearing as soon as possible.
   c. Discharge the employee for falsification of the application.
   d. Make the employee aware of the discovery but take no formal disciplinary action.

106. What is the most prevalent problem associated with the use of employee attitude surveys?
   a. Surveys are administered in-house.
   b. Employees are informed of survey results.
   c. Survey results are not responded to by management.
   d. Surveys are administered prior to management perceiving a problem.

107. A selection test for firefighters that requires all applicants to pull a 90-pound hose up three flights of stairs within a four-minute period would suggest which type of validity?
   a. Predictive.
   b. Concurrent.
   c. Content.
   d. Construct.

108. A primary employer advantage of implementing a skill-based pay system is:
   a. increased compensation costs.
   b. increased employee productivity.
   c. reduction of training and development expenses.
   d. ease of administration.

109. Greater flexibility for employees can be built into a vacation leave program by:
   a. providing more vacation time.
   b. reducing the advance notice period.
   c. allowing a carry-over of unused leave.
   d. having supervisors assign leave time.

110. A safety manager who wanted to know if financial incentives would reduce accidents randomly selected two departments and offered employees bonuses for reducing accidents. The incidence rates of these two departments were compared with other departments. This study illustrates what kind of experiment?
   a. Case study.
   b. Laboratory study.
   c. Field experiment.
   d. Simulation.

111. Which of the following common selection techniques is least predictive of workplace violence?
   a. Psychological Assessments
   b. Behavioral Interviews
   c. Reference Checks
   d. Criminal Records Review

112. The concept of trainee involvement and immediate feedback are most prominent in which of the following training methods?
   a. Lecture.
   b. Correspondence courses.
   c. Programmed instruction.
   d. Audiovisual techniques.

113. In an arbitration proceeding, it is agreed by all parties that the action complained about is a very slight departure from what is required in the labor contract. In such a case, the arbitrator is most likely to present the rule of:
   a. reason.
   b. parole evidence.
   c. de minimis.
   d. management by exception.

114. The most adequate defense an employer has in a defamation of character lawsuit arising from providing reference information is:
   a. the absence of malice.
   b. that the information given was the truth.
   c. that the employer had a qualified privilege to provide the information.
   d. that the employee signed a release.

115. In an organization adopting a pay-for-performance philosophy:
    a. a greater amount of employee pay is "at risk."
    b. cost of living increases are commonplace.
    c. length of service is used in calculating pay increases.
    d. external competitiveness dominates compensation decisions.

116. Which of the following activities of a firm would NOT be part of its social responsibility?
    a. Corporate giving.
    b. Environmental protection.
    c. Civil Rights Act compliance.
    d. Diversity training.

117. For a training program designed to enhance group problem-solving skills, which type of seating management is most appropriate?
    a. Classroom style.
    b. Chevron style.
    c. Circle style.
    d. Theater style.

118. The least serious OSHA violation is:
    a. other than serious.
    b. de minimis.
    c. serious.
    d. willful and repeated.

119. Which of the following cannot be included in a salesperson's deductions for travel expenses for federal income tax purposes?
    a. Meal expenses.
    b. Lodging expenses.
    c. Entertainment expenses.
    d. Home-to-work commuting allowances.

120. Under the Drug-Free Workplace Act (1988), an employer with government contracts worth more than $25,000 must do all of the following EXCEPT:
    a. terminate employees for off-time job drug usage.
    b. inform employees of drug-free requirements.
    c. outline actions to be taken.
    d. establish awareness programs and supervisory training.

121. In developing an international HR program, which factor is most critical to the success of an expatriate assignment in a foreign country?
    a. Equalizing negative tax consequences.
    b. Adaptation of spouse and family to a foreign country.
    c. Providing for security of expatriate and family.
    d. Readjustment training upon repatriation.

122. When a grievance goes to final and binding arbitration, arbitrators base their decisions on:
    a. their interpretation of the language of the labor agreement.
    b. the intent of the parties when the labor agreement was negotiated
    c. past arbitration dealing with the same issue in different organizations.
    d. the position of the National Labor Relations Board on the issue.

123. Tests would likely be used for evaluating the results of training programs when which criterion is utilized?
    a. Reaction.
    b. Learning.
    c. Behavior.
    d. Results.

124. A medical exam as part of the selection process should be:
    a. conducted prior to making the selection decision.
    b. scheduled after an employment offer has been extended.
    c. eliminated as a result of the Americans With Disabilities Act.
    d. conducted on a random basis.

125. Which of the following presents the least ethical dilemma for an HR manager to address?
    a. Specifically excluding salaries of low-paying organizations from a survey of HR positions.
    b. Referring a qualified personal friend's resume for an open position in another department.
    c. Informing employees of the reasons for the dismissal of a co-worker.
    d. Discussing an injured employee's medical condition with co-workers.

End of Sample Questions

Quick Scoring Key

Number	Answer	Topic Area	Number	Answer	Topic Area
1.	B	02-03	37.	A	05-07
2.	A	01-06	38.	B	05-02
3.	B	03-04	39.	A	04-07
4.	B	05-09	40.	A	02-04
5.	B	04-11	41.	B	03-02
6.	A	02-08	42.	B	05-01
7.	D	06-09	43.	C	01-01
8.	D	05-02	44.	B	04-01
9.	B	03-04	45.	B	02-06
10.	B	02-09	46.	D	02-06
11.	A	05-09	47.	A	05-01
12.	C	01-02	48.	A	02-08
13.	A	03-01	49.	C	04-10
14.	D	04-06	50.	D	01-06
15.	A	04-02	51.	D	01-06
16.	C	02-08	52.	A	03-03
17.	D	05-01	53.	B	02-16
18.	D	01-02	54.	B	05-10
19.	B	05-01	55.	A	04-01
20.	A	04-02	56.	B	04-06
21.	C	02-08	57.	C	02-02
22.	A	03-06	58.	C	01-06
23.	A	02-08	59.	C	03-03
24.	C	05-09	60.	B	05-10
25.	A	04-08	61.	C	01-07
26.	A	03-06	62.	C	04-02
27.	A	04-01	63.	C	02-14
28.	B	05-09	64.	B	06-01
29.	B	01-01	65.	B	05-01
30.	B	02-17	66.	C	02-02
31.	A	04-06	67.	A	02-13
32.	B	01-06	68.	D	05-04
33.	C	03-03	69.	B	02-06
34.	C	06-10	70.	B	05-10
35.	B	03-14	71.	C	04-03
36.	C	04-01	72.	D	03-03

Number	Answer	Topic Area	Number	Answer	Topic Area
73.	B	04-01	111.	A	06-11
74.	B	02-09	112.	C	03-03
75.	A	05-02	113.	C	05-10
76.	A	03-01	114.	B	02-09
77.	D	05-08	115.	A	04-02
78.	A	06-08	116.	C	01-07
79.	A	04-08	117.	C	03-03
80.	D	05-01	118.	B	06-01
81.	B	04-01	119.	D	04-01
82.	B	02-03	120.	A	05-04
83.	C	04-03	121.	B	02-12
84.	A	03-02	122.	A	05-08
85.	B	01-09	123.	B	03-02
86.	B	03-13	124.	B	02-10
87.	C	05-10	125.	B	01-09
88.	C	02-09			
89.	A	01-06			
90.	A	04-01			
91.	A	03-04			
92.	D	03-13			
93.	A	04-02			
94.	C	02-09			
95.	C	04-02			
96.	D	03-11			
97.	A	01-03			
98.	C	05-02			
99.	D	04-02			
100.	D	02-08			
101.	C	03-03			
102.	A	02-08			
103.	B	05-02			
104.	B	03-12			
105.	D	05-07			
106.	C	05-03			
107.	C	02-04			
108.	B	04-02			
109.	C	04-08			
110.	C	06-07			

Functional Area:

01   Strategic Management

02   Workforce Planning and Employment

03   Human Resource Development

04   Compensation and Benefits

05   Employee and Labor Relations

06   Occupational Health, Safety and Security

Answers, Rationales and Coding

1. **Answer: b. Locker room attendant.**
   A Bona Fide Occupational Qualification (BFOQ) is a limited exception to the anti-bias rules under the Civil Rights Act, the Age Discrimination in Employment Act and the Americans With Disabilities Act. A BFOQ may be established on the basis of religion, sex, or national origin or absence of disability if the requirement is necessary to the normal operations of a business. This is a strict burden of proof that falls to the employer. It is not available with respect to race or color. The locker room attendant requires monitoring of locker rooms designated for one sex. Based upon community standards, a specific sex could probably be specified and supported.
   CODE: 02-03

2. **Answer: a. Industrial Relations Director.**
   An Industrial Relations Director is responsible for only labor relations and safety functions. The other positions are responsible for all major HR functions.
   CODE: 01-06

3. **Answer: b. Training department's overhead.**
   The training department's overhead is an indirect cost spread out over all training programs. All other options are direct costs associated with a single training program.
   CODE: 03-04

4. **Answer: b. The union seeking certification must represent only guards.**
   Due to divided loyalties and a conflict of interest, the NLRB has determined that plant guards must be in a separate union from other plant employees. During a strike situation, guards are responsible for protecting company property. Separating the guards into a different bargaining unit helps alleviate this problem.
   CODE: 05-09

5. **Answer: b. The principal residence is in the United States.**

The Internal Revenue Service allows home travel expenses to be deducted from taxes but only if the travel was to the expatriate's principal residence within the United States. Other locations are not tax deductible.

CODE: 04-11

6. **Answer: a. Past performance.**

Industrial psychologists have an axiom that the best indicator or prediction of future performance is past performance. The more recent the past performance, the stronger the predictive value. The more long term the past performance, the stronger the predictive value.

CODE: 02-08

7. **Answer: d. Treatment outcome.**

Most employee assistance programs provide periodic reports to employers outlining program activity. To protect employee confidentiality, information is compiled in such a way to guarantee anonymity. Treatment outcome is almost never reported back to the employer. The other information—initial diagnosis category, referral source and utilization—is typically found in EAP provider reports.

CODE: 06-09

8. **Answer: d. Direct discussions between supervisors and employees.**

Personal communication between employees and supervisors is the most effective upward communication format. Research shows that competent first-line supervisors are critical for management to feel the pulse of the organization. While the other forms of upward communication may be valuable, they are less effective than personal communication between supervisors and employees.

CODE: 05-02

9. **Answer: b. Human relations.**

All of the options except human relations can be objectively measured and quantified. Soft skills, such as human relations, can be observed but represent a challenge in terms of measurement.

CODE: 03-04

10. **Answer: b. Do you have a job-related disability?**

Under the Americans With Disabilities Act (ADA), pre-employment inquiries about a disability are unlawful. The ADA requires a focus on essential job functions and whether the person can perform those functions with or without reasonable accommodations.

CODE: 02-09

11. **Answer: a. Win a majority of the votes cast in an election.**

Much like political elections in the United States, the NLRB requires a union to win a majority of the votes during a representation election in order to certify the union. It is important, then, that all eligible employees participate in the voting so a small minority does not determine the fate of many.

CODE: 05-09

12. **Answer: c. Labor market.**

All of the options are areas searched in an environmental scan. The three factors listed are all factors of the relevant labor market.

CODE: 01-02

13. **Answer: a. Conducting a job/task analysis.**

A basic way to ensure content validity of training programs is to conduct a job/task analysis. The other options are less related to content validity.

CODE: 03-01

14. **Answer: d. They overestimate the pay of their peers and underestimate that of their supervisors.**

Research (Lawler, 1972; Milkovich and Anderson, 1972) indicates that employees overestimate the pay of their peers and underestimate the pay of supervisors. The greater the overestimation, the greater the level of dissatisfaction with pay. As a result of this research, more organizations are moving away from pay secrecy to more open pay systems.

CODE: 04-06

15. **Answer: a. 6.25%**

Count up the remaining months of the increase for January (12), March (10), July (6), and November (2) (equals 30 months at $100 month). Divide $3,000 by the total starting payroll costs $48,000. The increase is 6.25%.

CODE: 04-02

16. **Answer: c. Reference checking.**

Negligent hiring is a tort law theory which holds that if an employer who hired an employee knew (or should have known) about a prior behavior of the employee that could cause harm to a third party, then the employer is liable if the employee subsequently causes harm to someone. Negligent hiring makes it extremely important for employers to thoroughly check background references on all employees who are in a position of trust or where their actions could harm others.

CODE: 02-08

17. **Answer: d. 100.**

The EEOC requires all employers with 100 or more employees to annually file an EEO-I report. The report numbers vary by type of organization.

EEO-1 Private Business

EEO-2 Joint Apprenticeship Committees

EEO-3 Unilateral Apprenticeship Programs

EEO-4 State and Local Governments

EEO-5 Public Elementary and Secondary Schools

EEO-6 Colleges and Universities

CODE: 05-01

18. **Answer: d. Determining the relationship between personnel demand and the firm's output.**

The demand for human resources is often directly related to the expected demand for the firm's products and/or services. In addition, the organization's objectives and productivity are important determinants.

CODE: 01-02

19. **Answer: b. Ensure the selection of trainees is well documented and does not result in adverse impact.**

Training is a condition of employment subject to EEO laws. As such, participation opportunities come under the Uniform Guidelines for Employee Selection Procedures (especially when training opens up promotional opportunities). Adverse impact calculations should be made on selection of trainees using the 4/5's rule.

CODE: 05-01

20. **Answer: a. The company does not do much advertising.**

    Sales compensation is a function of identifying customers, persuading customers, and servicing customers. The more customer identification, often known as prospecting, that is involved, the greater the incentive opportunity should be available. Organizations that do little advertising require more prospecting.

    CODE: 04-02

21. **Answer: c. Examining each item and determining to what extent it helped to predict job success.**

    An employment application form is considered a selection device under the Uniform Guidelines for Employee Selection Procedures. As such, if its use results in adverse impact, it should be evaluated. The best approach is to validate it to job performance.

    CODE: 02-08

22. **Answer: a. It permits employers to predict which additional skills are needed for the workforce of the future.**

    A skills inventory is a listing of the skills, knowledge, abilities and special qualifications of all employees in an organization. Employers can use skills inventories to determine long-range recruiting, selection and training needs. It is a critical aspect of workforce planning.

    CODE: 03-06

23. **Answer: a. Aptitude.**

    Interest tests such as the Strong-Campbell Interest Blank and the Kuder Preference Record are helpful in making selection and training decisions. They are also quite useful for counseling purposes. Personality inventories such as the Minnesota Multiphasic Personality Inventory measure some aspects of total personality. Specific abilities tests are used to measure a learned skill or knowledge about a specific occupation.

    CODE: 02-08

24. **Answer: c. Organizational opposition to unions.**

An organization can legally state opposition to the unionization of employees. A pay increase for remaining nonunion is a promise that constitutes an unfair labor practice. Likewise, a plant closure is a threat and also an unfair labor practice if done only to avoid the union. Endorsement of a specific union is also an unfair labor practice that could be construed as setting up a "company union."

CODE: 05-09

25. **Answer: a. Allow employees to contribute pretax dollars to buy additional benefits.**

The primary benefit of a flexible benefit plan involves favorable tax treatment under the Internal Revenue Code. Employees are able to use pretax dollars to purchase additional benefits.

CODE: 04-08

26. **Answer: a. Fall within perceptual and comprehension spans of the learners.**

Targeting content and training methods to the intended audience is critical to the success of training programs. Although culture, instructor, capability, and post-training transference are important, failure to accommodate the learners' capabilities affects training success more.

CODE: 03-06

27. **Answer: a. 2 years.**

The FLSA has a two-year statute of limitation for recovery of back pay. In cases of a willful or intentional violation, a three-year statute of limitation is available. Records should be kept for this three-year period unless state law requires a more stringent standard.

CODE: 04-01

28. **Answer: b. Inform the employees that he or she believes the international union may attempt to control local membership.**

Employers are free to educate employees as long as they do not spy, threaten, coerce or promise. Employers can make speeches to employees (captive audiences), but not within 24 hours of an election. Visiting the homes of employees and one-on-one discussions in management offices are clearly out of bounds.

CODE: 05-09

29. **Answer: b. Determine the information needs.**

An HRIS supports organizational decision-making; therefore, the first step is to determine the specific information needs. The other options, while important, should follow the information needs analysis.

CODE: 01-01

30. **Answer: b. Their availability in the reasonable recruitment area.**

The Office of Federal Contract Compliance Programs defines underutilization in relation to "the government contractor's reasonable recruitment area." That area involves where the contractor recruits or could be expected to recruit.

CODE: 02-17

31. **Answer: a. Offer incentive bonuses and stock ownership plans.**

Incentive bonuses and stock plans both focus employee behavior on building the company. They allow employees to share in the success of the company. High fixed-cost compensation programs are not appropriate for startup organizations.

CODE: 04-06

32. **Answer: b. Two organizational structures exist at the same time.**

With a matrix organizational structure, two organizational structures exist at the same time—a conventional functional organization and a project team organization. Employees join a project team but retain their positions in the conventional organization. Matrix structures are often prevalent in new product development.

CODE: 01-06

33. **Answer: c. Trainee hours lost from production.**

Time away from the job represents a significant cost of training programs for employees. Work goes undone, supervisors or co-workers fill in or overtime is incurred due to absences due to training. These expenses generally far exceed other training-related costs.

CODE: 03-03

34. **Answer: c. Document the situation before discussing the decreased performance with the employee.**

In general, supervisors are ill-equipped to handle alcohol-related problems in the workplace. They should not confront nor counsel someone suffering from alcoholism, but should address the situation as a performance problem and refer the employee to professional help.

CODE: 06-10

35. **Answer: b. Valuing differences.**

Diversity programs help employees understand, appreciate and value others who may be different than themselves. It represents a culture change away from ethnocentrism and exclusivity toward inclusiveness and community.

CODE: 03-14

36. **Answer: c. Direct the work of at least two other full-time employees.**

Under the FLSA, an executive must have as primary management duties: the supervision of two or more full-time employees, routinely exercise discretion, have authority to hire or fire, spend less than 20% of his or her time on nonexempt work, and be paid a salary of $155 per week or more.

CODE: 04-01

37. **Answer: a. An ad hoc arbitrator.**

An ad hoc arbitrator sits on a per-case basis. An interest arbitrator is used not in grievance but in collective bargaining. A permanent umpire serves as an arbitrator for the life of the labor contract. A tri-partite arbitrator is really an arbitration panel of three persons that may be ad hoc or permanent in nature.

CODE: 05-07

38. Answer: b. Value group norms and goals.

Sometimes cohesive groups value group norms and goals in detrimental ways, such as the "group think" phenomena. However, a cohesive group is generally easier to lead to goal attainment.

CODE: 05-02

39. Answer: a. Require contributions by the employee who will benefit from the income upon retirement.

Contributory pension plans require contributions by the employee who will benefit from the income upon retirement. Noncontributory pension plans do not require any contributions by employees. Noncontributory pension plans are popular because employees do not receive tax breaks on current earnings on contributions they make and tax laws create administrative burdens on plans that permit employee contributions.

CODE: 04-07

40. Answer: a. Competencies required and how they are assessed and maintained.

Because of the changing nature of virtual jobs, the traditional emphasis on knowledge, skills and abilities and essential job functions is not flexible enough to meet the requirements of the virtual workplace where multifaceted competencies determine success.

CODE: 02-04

41. Answer: b. Integrated with their experience.

Adult learning differs from other forms of learning in that trainee experience can be integrated into the learning process to make the learning process more meaningful. Traditional learning models such as classroom lecture and programmed instruction do not allow the flexibility of experiential development.

CODE: 03-02

42. **Answer: b. An auditor who performs a two-week audit of the company's financial records each year.**

The Internal Revenue Service has established a 20-factor test in making an independent contractor determination. Primary factors include: does the individual own his or her own facilities or equipment? Is there an opportunity to make a profit or loss? Are the services available to others? How much supervision is exercised?

CODE: 05-01

43. **Answer: c. Infrequently, once every seven to 10 years.**

Changes to organizational culture should not be undertaken often. Such changes should be thoroughly researched, planned and implemented over a period of years. This is especially true for more stable organizations.

CODE: 01-01

44. **Answer: b. $364.48.**

In calculating overtime, incentive/bonus money is figured in the regular pay rate to determine the overtime rate (1.5 times base). Calculation is 42 hours x $8/hr = $336 for regular base rate. Overtime rate is $336 plus $20 = $356 ($8.48/hr) x 0.5 or $4.23/hr (premium rate) x 2 hours of overtime for a total premium pay of $8.48. Total compensation is $336 base rate plus $20 bonus plus $8.48 equals $364.48

CODE: 04-01

45. **Answer: b. Where it results in an undesirable status quo of an underrepresented workforce.**

Recruitment by "word of mouth" through current employees may create EEO problems. An underrepresented workforce will usually refer applicants like the workforce itself. The effect of such recruitment is to perpetuate past discrimination.

CODE: 02-06

46. **Answer: d. Examine the referral documents as to dates referred and pay the fee to the agency whose referral was received first.**

Although the other options all seem plausible, the HR manager is faced with an issue of contract law. The rule of thumb is that the first to refer receives the fee. Most agency contracts contain language to that effect.

CODE: 02-06

47. **Answer: a. Decline the request.**

Under Section 8 of the National Labor Relations Act (Wagner Act), it is an unfair labor practice for an employer to dominate or interfere with the information or administration of any labor organization or to contribute financial or other support to it. The use of company vehicles would be viewed as supporting the union.

CODE: 05-01

48. **Answer: a. Self-nomination.**

While the cost of assessing every person at particular levels may be prohibitive, reliance on supervisors to nominate participants also presents difficulties. Employee attributes considered important at higher levels may not be valued by supervisors in lower levels of the firm.

CODE: 02-08

49. **Answer: c. Money that is paid on a regular basis, but that must be earned from commissions or paid back.**

A draw is an amount advanced and repaid from future commissions. A draw system allows salespersons to even out compensation between high and low sales periods. A risk to employers is that future commission may not be large enough to cover the draw.

CODE: 04-10

50. **Answer: d. III, II, I, IV.**

Much like setting the temperature on a thermostat, the HR control process involves setting expectations/standards, observing/measuring performance, comparing actual to expected performance, and taking corrective action if necessary.

CODE: 01-06

51. **Answer: d. Utility analysis.**

A utility analysis builds an economic or statistical model to identify the costs and benefits associated with specific HR programs or activities. Utility analysis is one of the basic ways to establish the worth of HR programs.

CODE: 01-06

52. **Answer: a. Decision-making.**

Simulation and gaming is used most often to improve decision-making. Simulation is a development that requires the trainee to analyze a situation and decide a best course of action based on the data given.

CODE: 03-03

53. **Answer: b. The ratio of separations to total workforce.**

The Department of Labor approved the following formula for calculating turnover:

$$\frac{\text{Number of Terminations x 100}}{\text{Average Number of Employees}}$$

Turnover rates should be calculated for more fuller understanding. Rates can be calculated by facility, department, longevity, performance level, demographic group, etc., for a more detailed analysis of turnover pockets.

CODE: 02-16

54. **Answer: b. Continue its practice and negotiate.**

Coffee breaks are a mandatory subject for negotiation. However, the employer is under no obligation to change past practice until the item has been negotiated. Unions often attempt to change past practice outside of the bargaining environment. The employer's best strategy is to deal with the issue through the formalized structure of collective bargaining.

CODE: 05-10

55. **Answer: a. Employees with less than one year of service.**

Under ERISA, a party-in-interest includes all individuals who come under or have impact on a qualified plan. Owners, trustees, administrators, etc., are all considered a party-in-interest. Until an individual becomes a plan participant, he or she is not considered a party-in-interest.

CODE: 04-01

56. **Answer: b. The mix between indirect and direct compensation.**

Although all options are important to designing and administering employee benefit plans, only the mix between indirect compensation (benefits) and direct compensation (pay) can be controlled by the organization. The mix becomes an important element in a total compensation or rewards strategy.

CODE: 04-06

57. **Answer: c. Questionnaire.**

Questionnaires, as a means of gathering job-analysis data, provide the most efficient use of resources when data must be collected on many jobs. Questionnaires are self-administered, allowing them to be given to many participants at once. They may be open-ended to allow great flexibility or highly structured to fit compensation or validation needs. Observation is very time-consuming, especially for long cycle jobs. Likewise, individual interviews require quite a bit of time. Functional job analysis, used by the federal government, is highly structured and requires extensive resources.

CODE: 02-02

58. **Answer: c. A formal research effort to evaluate the current state of human resource management within the organization.**

An HR audit is a systematic study of the HR functions performed—or not performed—in the organization and identifies strengths, weaknesses and corrective action.

CODE: 01-06

59. **Answer: c. The instructor must select a case with which the training group can identify.**

Case studies represent an excellent form of development as long as learning transfer back to the workplace takes place. A key factor in this transferability is the relevance of the case situation and trainee identification with the case.

CODE: 03-03

60. **Answer: b. Meet and discuss those mandatory items brought up by the other side.**

Good-faith bargaining does not require either side to agree to anything. The only requirement is that they meet and discuss the mandatory issues raised by the other side. Good faith is measured by the totality of the conduct of the party.

CODE: 05-10

61. **Answer: c. Sensitivity training.**

Organizational development (OD) is designed to increase an organization's effectiveness through planned interventions using behavioral science knowledge. A number of techniques are used in OD, including sensitivity training. This method makes individuals aware of themselves and the impact they have on others. Sensitivity training features an unstructured group with no specific agenda. The interaction that takes place in these groups is apparently quite threatening to some people.

CODE: 01-07

62. **Answer: c. Professional personnel**

Maturity curves are a compensation plan that depicts the relationship between experience in a career field and pay level. They are most appropriate to professionals in science, engineering, architecture and related fields.

CODE: 04-02

63. **Answer: c. Both indirect and direct costs.**

In calculating total organizational hiring costs, all costs associated with turnover must be considered. Down time, lost productivity, and training time are a few of the cost factors that must be considered.

CODE: 02-14

64. **Answer: b. Establish a written exposure control plan.**

The OSHA Bloodborne Pathogens Standard requires employers subject to OSHA that have any employees with on-the-job exposure to blood or other bodily fluids to take the following steps:

1. Establish a written exposure control plan.
2. Observe universal precautions.
3. Identify and adopt engineering and work practice controls.
4. Provide personal protective equipment.
5. Develop housekeeping, waste management and laundry standards.
6. Make available free hepatitis B vaccinations to those employees with occupational exposure.
7. Establish post-exposure evaluation.
8. Communicate hazards to employees.
9. Maintain specific record keeping.

CODE: 06-01

65. **Answer: b. Sixty days notice if a mass layoff or facility closing is to occur.**

WARN was intended to provide affected workers, their union (if present), elected public officials and state employment services advance notice of impending mass layoffs and/or plant closings. Nothing in WARN requires severance pay, re-education or retraining allowances, or disclosure of the circumstances regarding the layoff or closing.

CODE: 05-01

66. **Answer: c. The job itself.**

Motivation can be categorized as extrinsic or intrinsic. Extrinsic motivation comes from the environment—pay, working conditions and supervision. Intrinsic motivation comes from within the employee—the work, challenge, and curiosity.

CODE: 02-02

67. **Answer: a. Be modularized and spread out over a period of time.**

Too much information given too fast creates information overload and reduces information retention. To minimize this problem, orientation activities should be divided into manageable units and spread out over time.

CODE: 02-13

68. **Answer: d. Rule is reasonably related to a legitimate business reason.**

Work rules cannot be arbitrary and capricious. They must relate to a legitimate business reason in order to be upheld.

CODE: 05-04

69. **Answer: b. It establishes an ongoing professional relationship that enables positions to be filled more efficiently.**

There are two types of executive search firms—contingency firms and retainer firms. Contingency firms charge a fee only after a candidate is hired by a client. Retained firms charge a set fee whether or not a contracted search has been successful. The ongoing relationship with a retained firm is a primary benefit over a contingency firm. Both types of firms are ethically bound not to approach current employees of clients.

CODE: 02-06

70. **Answer: b. Provide the supervisor's salary schedule to the union.**

Management has a duty to provide relevant information to a union for collective bargaining purposes. Determining what is relevant is often problematic. If a rationale for not granting a pay increase involves a pay compression problem with supervisors, the union is entitled to such information. If management did not use this rationale, it would be under no obligation to provide the supervisor's salary schedule.

CODE: 05-10

71. **Answer: c. Income level.**

For compensation purposes, a relevant labor market is defined as the market from which an organization secures new employees from or to which they lose current employees. Income level is not a traditional labor market for survey purposes, whereas geographic, skill and industry represent relevant defined labor markets.

CODE: 04-03

72. **Answer: d. Role-play.**

Role-play requires the trainee to assume a role in a mock situation and act out that role. It is behavioral-based and allows for feedback on the trainee's performance. Discipline and discharge training is ideally suited for role-playing.

CODE: 03-03

73. **Answer: b. The plan must not discriminate in favor of highly compensated executives.**

The Internal Revenue Service has stated that for a benefits plan to qualify for tax-favored status, it must be a definite written plan and arrangement that is communicated to the employees and established and maintained by an employer for the exclusive benefit of employees or beneficiaries. As such, the plan cannot discriminate in favor of certain highly compensated employees.

CODE: 04-01

74. **Answer: b. Multiple incumbent positions.**

Weighted applications are designed using job analysis and performance appraisal data. Certain responses are given weights or numerical scores based on performance data. Weighted applications are time-consuming and must be periodically validated the same as tests. Because of this, they are most appropriate for multiple incumbent positions.

CODE: 02-09

75. **Answer: a. Extinction.**

Extinction is ignoring behavior. Punishment includes sending the employee home until the hairstyle is changed. Negative reinforcement exists if the supervisor criticizes the hairstyle. Positive reinforcement involves the supervisor complimenting the employee on the hairstyle.

CODE: 05-02

76. **Answer: a. Job inventory questionnaire.**

Job inventory questionnaires can be administered to a large group of employees in a short amount of time to identify training needs. The other identified methods are more time-consuming.

CODE: 03-01

77. **Answer: d. A union representative may be present for investigative meetings that lead to discipline if requested by the employee.**

Under the Weingarten decision (*NLRB v. Weingarten, Inc.* 420 U.S. 262, 1974), the U.S. Supreme Court ruled that union representation must be given to an employee when the employee requests representation and he or she reasonably believes the investigation will result in disciplinary action.

CODE: 05-08

78. **Answer: a. Without regard to who is at fault.**

Workers' compensation is designed to provide no-fault coverage for work-related injuries and illnesses. The passage of workers' compensation statutes took away from employees the right to raise defenses of contributory negligence on the employee or co-worker's part and on the employer's part.

CODE: 06-08

79. **Answer: a. Require employees to work the day before and after a holiday to be eligible for holiday pay.**

The most common practice in traditional time-off plans is the requirement that employees work the last scheduled day before and after a holiday in order to minimize the use of unscheduled absence such as sick leave. Many employers allow for scheduled preapproved vacation days in conjunction with holidays to provide employees maximum use of available time off.

CODE: 04-08

80. **Answer: d. Hostile environment.**

Posting of pinups is an example of a hostile environment theory of sexual harassment. Under this theory, sexual harassment is not directed at one person but creates an environment that interferes with work performance. The use of sexually suggestive jokes can also be an example of the hostile environment theory. There are no employment conditions or consequences from the pinup.

CODE: 05-01

81. **Answer: b. It is equivalent to the number of hours worked overtime within the same workweek.**

Compensatory time off, or comp time, is time off given in lieu of payment of extra time worked. It is illegal in the private sector unless it is given at the rate of one and one-half times the base rate for hours worked in a 40-hour workweek. It may not be carried over beyond the pay period. In the public sector, for police and fire employees and limited other employees, comp time may be "booked" up to a set number of hours.

CODE: 04-01

82. **Answer: b. Driving.**

Asking about a driving record is legitimate if the future employee has to drive as part of his or her duties. Inquiries about workers' compensation may be illegal under the ADA. Inquiries about arrest records have a disproportionate impact on minority group members. Employers may not discriminate based upon union preference.

CODE: 02-03

83. **Answer: c. It is $25 higher.**

The unweighted average salary is

700 + 700 + 700 + 800(2,900) divided by 4 = $725.

The weighted average salary is calculated as follows:

        15 x 700 = 10,500
        10 x 700 = 7,000
        25 x 700 = 17,500
        50 x 800 = 40,000
        100   75,000 divided by 100 = $750

CODE: 04-03

84. **Answer: a. Expectancy theory.**

Reinforcement theory holds that the consequences of behavior influence that behavior. To be most effective, reinforcement must be provided as soon after the desired behavior as possible. Herzberg's motivation-hygiene theory focuses on satisfiers or motivators (such as achievement and responsibility), and dissatisfiers, or hygiene factors which are important in preventing "demotivation" but do not positively motivate performance. Hygiene factors are company policy, working conditions, and pay. Equity theory suggests that individuals compare their rewards and the efforts required to reach them with the rewards and efforts of other relevant individuals.

CODE: 03-02

85. **Answer: b. Task accomplishment.**

This item comes from leadership research from Ohio State that identified two leader behaviors of consideration and initiating structure: University of Michigan researchers who identified production-centered and employee-centered leadership; and the Blake and Mouton Managerial Grid, which uses as its dimensions concerns for the task and concern for people.

CODE: 01-09

86. **Answer: b. Criterion deficiency.**

Criterion deficiency occurs when significant aspects of job performance are not captured by the appraisal instrument. Criterion contamination occurs when the appraisal instrument captures irrelevant factors to performance. Rater bias is the prejudice of the rater that influences ratings. Contrast error is rating one employee higher or lower, not because of objective performance but because of how he or she compares to another employee.

CODE: 03-13

87. **Answer: c. Helping companies and unions to reach agreement during contract negotiations.**

The Federal Mediation and Conciliation Service (FMCS) assists union/management negotiations when an impasse is reached. The FMCS attempts to keep the parties talking by finding common ground for further discussion. It tries to forestall a strike or lockout.

CODE: 05-10

88. **Answer: c. The employee should be fired for falsification of the application.**

A commonly recognized principle-at-law is that fraudulent misrepresentation on an application is grounds for immediate dismissal. Additionally, falsification of official records is viewed as a serious violation of work rules. If an applicant intentionally lies or conceals information and was previously terminated by another employer for misconduct, it is safe to assume that additional problems will occur. The best indicator of future performance is past performance. The employee should be terminated.

CODE: 02-09

89. **Answer: a. Organizational culture supports the TQM program.**

Research shows the number one determinant of success in a total quality management program is support by all members of the organization. TQM is not a single technique, but a total philosophy for operating an organization. Although union acceptance of the TQM program and statistical aptitude of supervisors are factors that can affect success, they are far less important than organizational support.

CODE: 01-06

90. **Answer: a. Funding requirements.**

The Employee Retirement Security Act of 1974 (ERISA) was established to regulate various fringe compensation programs including medical, life and disability programs as well as pension programs. ERISA addresses employer reporting and disclosure, funding of benefits, fiduciary responsibilities and vesting rights.

CODE: 04-01

91. **Answer: a. Product knowledge.**

With differing experience levels among salesperson trainees, selling techniques would be a challenge for training. Most sales training programs with diverse participants focus on common content for trainees, in this case, product knowledge.

CODE: 03-04

92. **Answer: d. Halo/horned error.**

Allowing the rating of one area of performance to influence the rating of another area of performance is a criterion contamination problem frequently referred to as the halo/horned effect. If the influence is positive, it is the halo effect. If the influence is negative, it is the horned effect. Leniency is rating all employees very high. Its opposite is strictness or rating all employees very low. Central tendency involves rating persons in a narrow band in the middle of a rating scale. Rater bias occurs when a rater's values or prejudices distort the ratings.

CODE: 03-13

93. **Answer: a. Least squares method.**

The least squares method of regression analysis is a technique for fitting a line to data plotted on a graph to determine the degree of correlation (or significance) between two variables. In building a salary structure, the plotted line is referred to as the trend line and salary grades are based on it.

CODE: 04-02

94. **Answer: c. Nondirective interviewing technique.**

A nondirective interview uses general open-ended questions from which other probing questions can be asked. Nondirective interviews are less threatening to the interviewee and allow a broader discussion. A potential difficulty associated with nondirective interviews involves obtaining standardized information from interviewees.

CODE: 02-09

95. **Answer: c. Merit increases that reward existing employees for higher productivity.**

Pay compression exists when pay differentials between new hires and long-term employees are small or when pay differentials between supervisors and those supervised are small. Merit increases very seldom cause pay compression.

CODE: 04-02

96. **Answer: d. Graphic rating scales.**

Central tendency is a common problem associated with a performance appraisal that uses a graphic rating scale. The rater evaluates all employees as average or in the mid-range of the scale. In effect, the rater is not making any judgments.

CODE: 03-11

97. **Answer: a. Human resource planning is the essential component of strategic organizational planning.**

Human resource planning must flow from and complement strategic organizational planning. Strategic planning involves identifying organizational objectives and actions needed to achieve those objectives. Human resource planning involves analyzing the need for and availability (or unavailability) of human resources so that the organization can meet its objectives.

CODE: 01-03

98. **Answer: c. Maintain an open line of direct and factual communication with employees.**

Research consistently shows that many employees are uninformed and misinformed in most organizations. The most effective employee relations initiative of the options provided is in communication. First-line supervisors are the key to keeping the lines of communication both open and factual.

CODE: 05-02

99. **Answer: d. Freezing their salary until job grade maximum increases catch up with the red circle rate.**

A red circle rate is where the incumbent is paid above the rate range maximum for the job. Red circle rates come about either through the administration of a new job evaluation plan or when an employee may take a demotion. The standard practice for handling red circle rates is to freeze the incumbent's salary until such time as the range catches up to the rate.

CODE: 04-02

100. **Answer: d. Training performance.**

An aptitude test measures accumulated learning from a number of sources. It measures one's capability as it relates to training performance. Other tests are more appropriate at predicting the other options.

CODE: 02-08

101. **Answer: c. Simulation training.**

Simulation training uses a controlled training situation away from the work site. It provides realistic conditions in an environment where the consequences of errors can be minimized. Business cases and executive games are examples of simulations that are adaptable to planning and conceptual skills. Too often, simulation only brings to mind skill training such as drivers' education or flight training for pilots. The other options, sensitivity training, human relations training and role-playing are more appropriate techniques for personal interaction skills training.

CODE: 03-03

102. Answer: a. They assess "can do" rather than "will do."

Performance is a function of skills and abilities multiplied by motivation. Skill tests measure whether the person has the skills necessary to perform the job. They measure aptitude, which in turn serves as a measure of capability. Skill tests do not predict motivation, and are better at predicting failures rather than successes.

CODE: 02-08

103. Answer: b. Bandwidth time.

Bandwidth time refers to the total range of hours when employees can begin and end work. Core time refers to those hours when all employees must be at work. If an employee must work eight hours between 6:00 a.m. and 6:00 p.m., the time between 6:00 a.m. and 6:00 p.m. is referred to as bandwidth time.

CODE: 05-02

104. Answer: b. Developmental purposes.

Multisource assessments are also referred to as 360-degree feedback, full-circle feedback and multirater assessment. First, critical competencies, behaviors or values are identified. Then managers are evaluated on these skill sets by having direct reports, internal and external customers, peers or co-workers, or superiors complete a confidential survey about the person's ability. The summarized data is shared with the manager for developmental purposes. Multisource assessments are popular in team environments.

CODE: 03-12

105. Answer: d. Make the employee aware of the discovery but take no formal disciplinary action.

In this situation, the falsification occurred so long ago that it is highly unlikely an arbitration would uphold a grievance or termination. A "stale" past record serves to set aside any disciplinary action especially given a good current performance record.

CODE: 05-07

106. **Answer: c. Survey results are not responded to by management.**

Administering an attitude survey to employees implies that the results will be followed-up by management. If employees are to voluntarily partici-pate in such surveys, they must believe that the feedback will result in change. Research indicates that the failure to share results and respond to problems significantly reduces participation in subsequent surveys.

CODE: 05-03

107. **Answer: c. Content.**

Pulling a 90-pound hose up three flights of stairs represents an actual work sample for a firefighter. Work samples are the most basic form of content validity. The test in this instance measures an actual content domain of the job.

CODE: 02-04

108. **Answer: b. Increased employee productivity.**

The primary employer advantage is increased productivity from a higher-skilled workforce. Additionally, a skills-based pay system provides increased compensation to employees as they master and become certi-fied in new skills. These systems are person-based, as opposed to job-based. They pay for skill mastery as opposed to responsibility. These plans provide both job enrichment and job security for employees. They allow for the opportunity to earn more pay. In practice, payroll costs are less because of increased workforce flexibility and decreased staffing.

CODE: 04-02

109. **Answer: c. Allowing a carry-over of unused leave.**

Accrual of vacation leave along with year-end carry-over allows employ-ees to accumulate vacation leave for special occasions. If the amount of carry-over is great, it can create a cash flow problem for employers when taken or paid-out upon termination.

CODE: 04-08

110. **Answer: c. Field experiment.**

A field experiment involves manipulating an independent variable (financial incentives) and measuring the effect on a dependent variable (incident rates). A case study involves analyzing an event and describing what happened. A laboratory study and a simulation both occur in a controlled environment as opposed to a natural work environment.

CODE: 06-07

111. **Answer: a. Psychological Assessments**

Given what is known about violent behavior in the workplace, no psychological tests can adequately assess an employee's circumstances, feelings and thoughts to make an accurate prediction of how that person will behave. Well-designed job-related behavioral interview questions can predict violence potential when they assess past human relations skills, coping skills (i.e., stress tolerance) and organizational fit. Likewise, both reference checks and criminal records review are based upon the adage that the best indicator of future performance is past performance. Behavior has a strong tendency to repeat itself.

CODE: 06-11

112. **Answer: c. Programmed instruction.**

Programmed instruction typically provides a small amount of information to the trainee and then poses a question. If the correct answer is given, the trainee is dircted to the next "frame." If the incorrect response is given, the trainee is directed to restudy the information.

CODE: 03-03

113. **Answer: c. De minimis.**

Minor violations of a collective bargaining agreement are generally not accorded much weight by arbitrators. These "de minimis" violations, while technically wrong, do not generally result in substantial harm to either party. Only when a pattern of such "de minimis" violations is demonstrated will an arbitrator remedy in an award.

CODE: 05-10

114. Answer: b. That the information given was the truth.

The ultimate or absolute defense in a defamation of character suit is the truth. For a plaintiff to prevail, he or she must show that the information provided was a lie. Although the other options to this item are defenses, the truth provides the most protection for the employer.

CODE: 02-09

115. Answer: a. A greater amount of employee pay is "at risk."

Pay-for-performance systems are becoming very popular because of their perceived relationship to organizational performance. In a pay-for-performance system, no increases are given except when justified by objective measurable performance increases.

CODE: 04-02

116. Answer: c. Civil Rights Act compliance.

Social responsibility is the idea that business has social obligations above and beyond making a profit. It goes beyond complying with the law—in this case, the Civil Rights Act. It is voluntary actions that result from the business helping itself to ultimately help others.

CODE: 01-07

117. Answer: c. Circle style.

Circle and horseshoe seating arrangements are especially suited for highly interactive training such as group problem solving. Classroom, chevron and theater seating lend themselves to large group presentations with less trainer-participant interaction.

CODE: 03-03

118. Answer: b. De minimis.

OSHA categorizes violations in the following manner—de minimis, other than serious, serious, willful and repeated, and imminent danger. A de minimis violation does not have a direct and immediate relationship to the employee's health and safety. An other-than-serious violation could have an impact on the employee's health and safety, but would not cause death or serious harm and the employer should know the condition. Willful and repeated violations occur when the employer has previously been cited by OSHA for the same condition.

CODE: 06-01

119. **Answer: d. Home-to-work commuting allowances.**

The first three options are legitimate sales-related expenses that qualify under the Internal Revenue Codes as deductible expenses. Home-to-work travel is not a sales-related expense.

CODE: 04-01

120. **Answer: a. Terminate employees for off-time job drug use.**

The Drug-Free Workplace Act addresses only on-the-job drug use. Many employers refer employees with drug abuse problems to employee assistance programs or other professional treatment sources.

CODE: 05-04

121. **Answer: b. Adaptation of spouse and family to a foreign country.**

Although many factors affect the success of a foreign assignment, research consistently shows that the adjustment of spouse and family is the most critical factor. Employers too often do not give enough weight to this factor in developing their international HR programs. The focus tends to be on the expatriate and not his or her family.

CODE: 02-12

122. **Answer: a. Their interpretation of the language of the labor agreement.**

Arbitrators are bound by the four corners of the document, meaning they must interpret the specific language of the labor agreement. The labor agreement becomes controlling and the arbitration award is issued addressing the specific issue in question, under the specific clause of the labor agreement, in a specific organizational setting. As long as arbitrators act within the slope and bounds of their authority, their decisions cannot be successfully appealed in the judicial system.

CODE: 05-08

123. Answer: b. Learning.

Training reaction to the value of training programs is probably the most frequent criterion used to evaluate training programs. In this approach, trainees are asked (often using questionnaires) whether the training is useful. Learning is what trainees can demonstrate that they know as a result of the training. Using tests, it can be determined if they have learned successfully. When behavior is the criterion, the focus is on whether the learning will be applied on the job. Behaviors are most likely to be measured through a performance appraisal system such as BARS. Trainees may believe the training to be useful (reaction); they may even use newly acquired techniques on the job (behavior). However, organizations should be interested in results.

CODE: 03-02

124. Answer: b. Scheduled after an employment offer has been extended.

The Americans With Disabilities Act prohibits medical examinations before the extension of an employment offer. Results of a medical examination can then be used in making reasonable accommodations.

CODE: 02-10

125. Answer: b. Referring a qualified personal friend's resume for an open position in another department.

Although all the options are potential ethical dilemmas for the HR manager, referring the resume of a qualified friend to an open position in another department is the least problematic. As long as the HR manager does not advocate for the selection of the friend, no ethics violation would occur. To deny the referral based on friendship would deny a qualified candidate equal opportunity. Skewing salary survey data for self-betterment is clearly an ethics violation. Likewise, breaches of confidentiality are ethics violations.

CODE: 01-09

SECTION V:

Frequently Asked Questions

The following questions are those most frequently asked about HRCI and its certification program. The questions and answers are grouped into the following areas:

- Exam Application
- Exam Preparation
- HR Body of Knowledge
- The Certification Exams
- Exam Administration
- Recertification

Exam Application

Q. Why would my application be returned or rejected?

A. The most common reasons that applications are returned:

- No signature on application forms submitted by mail.
- Not including payment with the application.
- Sending a personal check rather than credit card payment (VISA, MasterCard, or American Express only), money order, cashier's check or organizational check.
- Not including supporting documentation, if needed.
- Submitting a faxed or photocopied application.
- Not including required forms if applicable, such as the student/ recent graduation verification form.

The most common reasons for rejecting an application are:
- Receiving the application after the late registration postmark date.
- Not having two years of exempt-level (professional) HR work experience.

Q. Are exam fees reduced for SHRM members?

A. Yes. HRCI is a separate organization from SHRM. However, SHRM founded HRCI and financially supported it for many years. Today, HRCI is self-supporting. The reduced exam fee for SHRM members is a professional courtesy to SHRM in appreciation for those early years of support.

Q. Why does HRCI require exempt-level (professional) HR work experience to be eligible to take the exam?

A. HRCI grants professional certification in the human resource management field. Certification is not granted for paraprofessional or other nonexempt experience. Candidates must have an executive, administrative, or professional exemption under the Fair Labor Standards Act to be eligible to take the PHR, SPHR or GPHR exam.

Q. Since the eligibility requirements are the same for the PHR and SPHR, how do I determine which exam to take?

A. If you have at least 2-4 years of exempt-level (professional) HR work experience, you should consider taking the PHR exam. If you have a broad range of experience/education and 6-8 years of experience, it might be appropriate to take the SPHR. The most important thing is to take the exam that best demonstrates your mastery of the domestic HR body of knowledge.

Exam Preparation

Q. What is the best way to prepare?

A. There is no single best way to prepare. A lot depends on your education and background in HR, your learning style and your lifestyle. Select a preparation method that best matches each of these areas. It might be a highly flexible approach such as individual self-study, or a moderately structured approach such as a preparation course or the SHRM® Learning System. In any case, remember that the exam tests your mastery of the HRCI body of knowledge and it is impossible to teach to the test. Candidates must master the HRCI test specifications and be able to apply those specifications.

Q. Does HRCI recommend learning resources?

A. No, HRCI does not endorse any one learning resource as being qualitatively better than another. At the same time, those resources based upon the HRCI test specifications may better prepare candidates for the tests.

Q. How do I know if I am ready to take the exam?

A. Review the HRCI test specifications. If you can honestly say that you are comfortable with each of the responsibilities and knowledge areas in the outline, you are probably a good candidate to take the exam. Consider taking a self-assessment exam to see how you perform.

HR Body of Knowledge

Q. Why are the HRCI test specifications so important?

A. Test specifications are the blueprint for the HRCI exams. The weightings on the specifications correspond to the weightings on the exam. Candidates will only be tested on subject matter included in the test specifications.

Q. How often does HRCI revise its test specifications?

A. The HR body of knowledge undergoes major revision every five years. Minor revisions occur annually as a result of expert or literature reviews.

The Certification Exams

Q. Where do the exam questions come from?

A. Test questions, or items, are written by certified HR professionals, not by academics or professional test developers. Because the questions are developed by certified HR professionals, they tend to be very practical and applied. HRCI exam scores correlate with years of experience and with education.

Q. How reliable are the exams?

A. Very reliable. If you do not pass an exam and decide to retake it without extensive preparation or additional experience, your results will be similar to the first time.

Q. Are HRCI exams validated?

A. Yes. HRCI exams are content validated. The blueprints for HRCI exams come from the HRCI test specifications. Those specifications are the result of the HRCI practice analysis process—a sort of job analysis for the entire HR field. Only questions that correspond to the test specifications are used on the exams. Contributing to this content validation model is the fact that HRCI uses only certified HR professionals to write items, review them, evaluate test forms, and analyze the performance of exams. HRCI test specifications conform to the highest standards in the certification testing field.

Q. What is the best predictor of success on the exam?

A. HR education and exempt-level (professional) work experience are the best predictors of success on the HRCI exams.

Q. What is the difference between a raw score and a scaled score?

A. A raw score is the actual number of items answered correctly on the exam. A scaled score is placed on a uniform scale and reflects differences in difficulty levels of different forms of the same exam. A scaled score ensures that every examinee, no matter when he or she took the exam, achieves the same uniform standard. A passing score on an HRCI exam is a scaled score of 500. This process ensures consistency and fairness between exam forms.

Q. Are certain functional areas of the exam more difficult than others?

A. The answer is based on the education and experience candidates bring to the exam. For instance, candidates who have never worked in a unionized environment could find items on employee and labor relations more difficult than those with experience in labor relations. It is really an individual matter. Each of the exam's functional areas include questions with a fairly broad range of difficulty levels.

Q. Why are PHR and SPHR exams weighted differently?

A. PHR and SPHR exams differ in terms of focus and cognitive level of questions. PHR exam questions tend to be at the operational/technical level, and the SPHR questions tend to be at the strategic and/or policy level. Therefore, a major emphasis on the SPHR exam is in strategic management.

Q. Are questions on the PHR exam different from those on the SPHR exam?

A. Yes. PHR questions tend to be technical and operational. They involve the cognitive abilities of recall and comprehension. SPHR questions tend to be more policy-oriented and strategic and test more of the ability to analyze and synthesize, often using scenario questions.

Q. What is a scenario question?

A. A scenario question includes a paragraph (called an information set) that provides basic information about a given situation. It is followed by a series of four answer multiple-choice items. Scenario questions are ideal for the SPHR exam because they require candidates to integrate information from more than one functional area of the test specifications to arrive at a correct answer. Scenario items reflect situations commonly encountered by senior-level HR practitioners.

Q. Do I have to memorize the year a law was passed?

A. The exams do not test trivia! It is not important to know what year (1935) the Wagner Act passed, but candidates should know how to identify an unfair labor practice. Remember—HRCI exam questions are very practical and applied.

Q. If I don't know the answer to a question should I leave it blank?

A. No. Scoring is based on the number of correct answers. A guess is far better than leaving a question blank.

Exam Administration

Q. I have a disability. Can I be accommodated at the exam site?

A. The HRCI certification program complies with the Americans With Disabilities Act covering both facilities and administration. Candidates with special accommodations should submit a request with supporting documentation to the HRCI test vendor at the time of application. Please see the HRCI *PHR and SPHR Certification Handbook* for more information about these procedures. Handbooks can be requested by calling (866) 898-4724 or viewed online at www.hrci.org.

Q. Do I need a calculator to take the exam?

A. Probably not. Exam questions are designed to be answered without a calculator. One will be available on the desktop of your computer, just in case.

Q. What should I do if I fail?

A. Start by reviewing your score report. All score reports show the raw scores (number correct) for each of the functional areas. This should help you identify areas that need improvement when considering additional preparation.

Q. Can I review my test booklet or get a list of the questions I missed?

A. Because of test security, test booklets and question/answer documents are not available for review. If you have questions about your exam, direct them to the HRCI exam vendor at the address in the HRCI *PHR and SPHR Certification Handbook*. All inquiries are reviewed.

Recertification

Q. How do I recertify?

A. Recertification is required every three years by the expiration date of the current certification cycle. Recertification can be achieved by successfully retesting or by documenting 60 contact hours of activities that update HR knowledge and/or experience.

Q. What education and experience counts toward the 60 recertification credit hours needed to recertify?

A. Activities in the following categories can count toward recertification:
- Continuing Education
- Research and/or Publishing
- Instruction
- On-the-Job Experience
- HR Leadership
- Professional Membership

Please visit the HRCI Web site at www.hrci.org for more information about the recertification process and for a recertification application form.

Q. How was the three-year time frame determined for recertification?

A. A recognition by the HRCI Board of the amount and speed of change occurring in the HR field.